TRANSFORMATIONS IN LITERATURE AND FILM

TRANSFORMATIONS IN LITERATURE AND FILM

Selected Papers from the Sixth Annual
Florida State University Conference
on Literature and Film

Edited by Leon Golden

A Florida State University Book

UNIVERSITY PRESSES OF FLORIDA

Tallahassee
1982

University Presses of Florida is the central agency
for scholarly publishing of the State of Florida's
university system. Its offices are located at 15
NW 15th Street, Gainesville, FL 32603. Works published by University Presses of Florida are evalu-
ated and selected for publication by a faculty edi-
torial committee of any one of Florida's nine public universities: Florida A&M University (Tallahassee), Florida Atlantic University (Boca Raton),
Florida International University (Miami), Florida
State University (Tallahassee), University of
Central Florida (Orlando), University of Florida
(Gainesville), University of North Florida (Jackson-
ville), University of South Florida (Tampa), University of West Florida (Pensacola).

Florida State University Conference on Literature
    and Film (6th : 1981)
    Transformations in literature and film.

    "A Florida State University book."
    Includes index.
    1. Moving-pictures and literature--Congresses.
I. Golden, Leon, 1930-   . II. Florida State
University. III. Title.
PN1995.3.F55 1981   700   82-20195
ISBN 0-8130-0744-5

PRINTED IN THE UNITED STATES OF AMERICA

CONTENTS

Preface

We are pleased to publish in this volume a se-
lection of papers from the sixth annual Florida
State University Conference on Literature and Film:
TRANSFORMATIONS IN LITERATURE AND FILM. These
papers intelligently and imaginatively illustrate
the breadth and depth of that conference as they
deal with the varied aesthetic, psychological, and
philosophical metamorphoses that take place within
literary and cinematic works and between literary
works and the films that are modeled on them. The
broad scope of these papers illustrates the special
virtue which we who sponsor these conferences see
in them. They offer a forum where critics as di-
verse as Aristotelians and Postmodernists can enter
into creative dialogue with one another and raise
each other's aesthetic consciousness. In an era of
increasing academic specialization we should not
undervalue experiences of this type.

We wish to express our gratitude here to a number of people who make this conference and its pro-
ceedings possible. First and foremost, of course
are the participants who provide the intellectual
substance of the conference. We are also grateful
to those who provide material support for these
conferences, without which they could not take
place. Florida State University's Vice President
for Academic Affairs, Augustus Turnbull, and its
Dean of the College of Arts and Sciences, Werner
Baum, have both supported the conference financial-
ly and have recognized its importance to the intellectual life of the university. The Departments of
Classics, English, and Modern Languages and Linguis-

Transformations in Literature and Film

tics have also made contributions to the conference
of the material and intellectual kinds. Finally,
our thanks go out to Diana Bourdon, who miraculously meets all impossible deadlines to produce the
pages for our annual conference volumes.

--L.G.

INTRODUCTION--TRANSFORMATIONS IN LIFE AND ART: FROM ARISTOTLE TO MARK HARRIS

Leon Golden

The term "transformation" has itself undergone a number of transformations since its appearance in the classical literature that begins the western literary tradition. The current volume, which focuses almost exclusively on twentieth-century works, indicates how varied and flexible a concept "transformation" has become. Some of the essays included here deal with transformations of a very traditional kind and reflect critical strategies that look back to Plato and Aristotle for their justification. Others are in open rebellion, as one of our authors suggests, against Aristotelian logic and the classical perception of reality, which remain an influential orthodoxy in our own time. We will be able to understand more clearly the world view of these essays if we measure them against the goals and demands of traditional Aristotelian aesthetics.

An orthodox Aristotelian, invited to participate in a conference on "Transformations in Literature and Film," would consider it his most important goal to define the essential nature of literature and film as art forms. He could begin his task confidently because of very specific statements made by Aristotle about the nature of mimetic art in general, which subsumes under it both literature and film. He would then outline what nuances and conno-

tations of "transformation" are possible in this
aesthetic context.

For an Aristotelian, the essential nature of art
in general and of all its various kinds is its character as mimesis, as "representation," which has as
its goal the illumination of the significant human
action that is the subject of the artistic mimesis.
An Aristotelian critic would point out that all such
representations can be analyzed in terms of the
means by which they carry out their mimetic task,
the objects which they represent, and the manner by
which they make themselves available to an audience.
Literature and film thus could share words, rhythm,
song, and meter as possible means while film could,
of course, claim cinematic imagery as powerful and
unique aesthetic means for itself. For an Aristotelian, both art forms represent as their object
human actions and characters that are either like
our own or better or worse than our own. Manner
refers to the way in which a work of art is presented to the public, with film requiring projec-
tion equipment and, usually, a theatre while literature uses whatever renders it accessible to an audience, usually a book or a theatre depending on the
genre we are discussing.

After identifying the learning experience that
arises from mimetic art as the highest and most
characteristically human pleasure, the Aristotelian
critic would then describe the conditions for
achieving this important goal of art. These re-
quirements center on the total control by the artist
of the elements of plot, character, thought, dic-
tion, melody, and spectacle that define the structure of both literature and film. Special emphasis,
however, must be placed on plot, which is the representation of human action, and character, which represents the moral and ethical choices made by human
beings.

Organization of the elements of mimesis in order
to achieve the required intellectual pleasure demands a plot that is complete in that it has a fully
appropriate beginning, middle, and end and also one
that has the proper magnitude, which means that the
represented action must be neither too short and
simple nor too long and complex. Under these re-
quirements, the mimesis must start at the natural
initiation of an action and proceed through a

causally connected middle to a necessary end. The
requirement of a proper magnitude means that the
plot must be sufficiently rich in detail and action
so as to engage fully the mind of the audience in a
persuasive and instructive way. Insufficient detail
will destroy persuasiveness, and thus ultimate clarification, while excessive detail will overwhelm the
mind of the audience and subvert the learning experience with confusion. Both the sequence of action
in the plot and the psychological unraveling of
character must be tightly governed by necessity and
probability, for only in this way can persuasive
instruction and clarification take place, which is
the essential goal of the mimesis. When an artistic
mimesis has been constructed according to necessity
and probability, it will achieve philosophical uni-
versality, illuminating many disparate particulars
and giving rise to the intellectual pleasure of the
learning experience.

For Aristotelian critics, then, all forms of art
are representations of human actions and each such
artistic representation must manifest organic unity
with its properly constructed beginning, middle, and
end neatly bonded by psychological and dramatic
necessity and probability. The ultimate goal and
essential telos of mimesis is the final cathartic
illumination that arises from the carefully structured, integrated, and unified representation that
is the successful work of art. We are caught up in
the profound intellectual pleasure of understanding
human action more fully than we did before our encounter with the work of art.

In the range of essays included in this volume we
find a number of affirmative relationships to Aristotelian theory as well as a number of radical di-
vergencies from it. These similarities and dissim-
ilarities illustrate the wide range of "transformations" that can take place in works of artistic
mimesis. The kind of transformation that takes
place in the Bildungsroman, a literary form which
Charlotte Goodman discusses in her paper, is probably closest in spirit to Aristotle's aesthetic
world view. At the core of the Bildungsroman is a
study of the evolutionary development of a protagonist or, in the case of the Bildungsromane written
by women novelists (which is the special subject of
Professor Goodman's investigation), the evolutionary

transformation of a pair of protagonists, one male
and one female. In such works as these there is a
clearly recognized need for a sharply etched beginning, middle, and end in the mimetically represented
human action and a highly appropriate opportunity
for character development to take place in accordance with the principles of psychological necessity
and probability. The developmental human action
leads inexorably to a universal statement, a cathartic illumination, that clarifies the destinies of
certain kinds of human beings under certain specified circumstances.

In this instance, Professor Goodman discovers
that the learning experience of Bildungsromane
written by women novelists arises from a "critique
of a society in which gender roles are rigidly
assigned" and is expressed in the message that the
"harmonious and balanced androgynous self is split
asunder by a world which insists that adult males
and females play radically different roles." In
structure and purpose, the Bildungsroman is fully
Aristotelian in its spirit and is ideally adapted
for carrying out the architectural plan for a work
of art that is outlined in the <u>Poetics</u>. The effectiveness, persuasiveness, and instructiveness of the
"Bildung" experience is dependent on our seeing that
the beginning, middle, and end of that experience
have indeed been governed by the laws of psychological necessity and probability and that the develop-
ments that have taken place have arisen organically
from the matrix of psychological, emotional, and
intellectual realities that define the personality
of the hero and heroine. The transformation involved here is one that arises through evolutionary
development in accordance with the rules of necessity and probability and reaches its climax in the
illumination of fate and character.

In Maurice Bennett's essay on Borges and Bergman,
the emphasis is on the transformation from the apparent to the real in the human soul, and Bennett's
intense concentration on diametrically opposed essential human truths conveyed by the two writers is
true to the Aristotelian insistence on cathartic
illumination as the goal of artistic mimesis. Unlike the Bildungsroman, the works with which Bennett
deals do not unravel their meaning through a real-
istically plotted human action. In the case of

Bergman, it is the graphic cinematic image, such as
the one in Persona in which the faces of two women
are combined into a single visage, and repeated symbolic events, such as the silence of one woman and
the ceaseless meaningless chatter of the other, that
are revelatory of the truth of human actions. In
works of this sort we deal with symbolic images and
events which, however, must also obey Aristotle's
rules of necessary and probable causality if they
are to persuade us of the truthfulness of their insights, and it is to such laws of internal psychological consistency that Bennett appeals in order
to select better symbolic interpretations over worse
ones.

The existential failures pictured in Bergman's
Persona are contradicted by Borges's world view,
and, again, symbolic interpretation as opposed to
the unraveling of plot is the mechanism of pene-
trating to the meaning of the artistic mimesis.
Bennett shows us how Borges creates a mythic symbol
that contradicts the destabilizing cult of self that
afflicts Bergman's world. This is a myth which by
recognizing the kinship of the individual with the
universe heals human anomie through a doctrine of
the cosmic unity of all things great and small.
Here, however, we are required to abandon the doctrines of necessity and probability which play such
an important role in Aristotelian aesthetics. Instead we must become Platonists, viewing ultimate
reality mythically through nous (mind) rather than
accepting the messages of aisthesis (sense perception), which delude and falsify. But both Bergman
and Borges transform symbol and myth into cathartic
illumination and are thus in harmony with the most
fundamental of all Aristotelian aesthetic doctrines.

Necessity, probability, and the orthodox clarification of human action are all totally denied in
the absurdist world view of Tardieu's Le Meuble, the
subject of Professor S. D. Henning's paper. Henning
points out that this work, which can be considered
an example of the grotesque, "unsettles the classical conception of teleological evolution according
to which things strive to embody as perfectly as may
be their specific form." On one level, the work
concerns the transformation of a mere machine into
a directing willful force and of the human intelli-
gence that invented it into the role of helpless

victim. But, on a larger scale, the transformation
that takes place in this work is a radical transformation of fundamental aesthetic purpose that
contradicts Aristotelian orthodoxy. The search for
meaning is still at the center of Hennings' interpretative strategy for dealing with Le Meuble, but
the meaning that emerges subverts the ordered and
logical structures that define the Aristotelian
world view. Things incompatible and contradictory
are joined together in this work in a new image of
reality that contradicts the laws of necessity and
probability and, as Henning says, "calls into question many of the basic concepts on which the classical perception of reality is grounded--a perception
which, to a large extent, is still our own."

Three other papers in this volume deal with the
question of the "real" or underlying or ultimate
meaning of a work of art as opposed to its surface
and apparent meaning and apply analytical strategies
that are designed to transform the surface meaning
into the underlying one. Professor Struebig applies
Lévi-Strauss's "law of myth" to Butor's La Modification and, treating that work as a contemporary myth
subject to Lévi-Strauss's formula, develops an
interpretative structure that illuminates the underlying meaning of the novel. Similarly, Professor
McManus discusses Bergman's Cries and Whispers in
reference to the psychoanalytical theme of the feminine archetype developed by Jung's student, Erich
Neumann. For McManus, the deeper meaning of the
Bergman film is illuminated through the interpretative use of its four female figures, who can be
subsumed under the female archetype. Professor
Petlewski shows us that a full reading of a genre
piece may require that we delve below the surface
into the subtext that is the "real" text. Here we
must become aware that although the surface patterns
of an ordinary western may be present in a work,
there may lie beneath those surface patterns a theme
of deeper significance for our interpretation of the
work. The authors of these three papers share with
Aristotle a fundamental concern with ultimate meaning but travel very different routes to that meaning
from Aristotle's concentration on the analysis of
plot and character.

Two papers in this volume deal with a question
that is obviously outside the realm of Aristotle's

concern, the transformation of a work of art from
literature into film. Professor Larsson deals with
the significant theoretical problems that exist
whenever such an act of transformation takes place.
He raises questions concerning the meaning of such
a transformation and what "accuracy" and "truthfulness" and "faithfulness" mean in regard to such
transformations. He, too, is concerned with Aristotelian illumination as he seeks a calculus for
evaluating the effectiveness of such transformations. He discusses the historical matrix within
which the text has its origin, its popular reception, its critical study, the aesthetic intent of
the adaptor in conjunction with market pressures to
produce a saleable commodity, and ideological con-
straints--both covert (manifested in sociological
and psychological subtexts) and overt (resulting
from direct pressures to bring a text into conformity with dominant moral and political practices as
these affect the direction taken by a given transformation).

Professor Pavlik, emphasizing form and structure,
deals specifically with the stream of films that
have been made using the Bible as their source and
shows how difficult it has been to bring off a
successful transformation of biblical episodes into
film. For one reason or another, filmmakers have
been unable to achieve an appropriate, intellectually satisfying plot magnitude or persuasive characterization in their translations of Biblical
stories, and their works often lack unity as well as
illumination. Without making specific reference to
Aristotle, Pavlik cites a number of structural weaknesses that also receive severe criticism in the
Poetics.

All of this leads us from Aristotle to Mark
Harris. We began by describing the Aristotelian
prescription for excellence in art--its emphasis on
a tightly knit structure of beginning, middle, and
end that is bound together by the laws of necessity
and probability and that leads to a powerful illumination, a catharsis, of the human action depicted in
the work of art. Mark Harris's description of the
making of most films provides a direct contradiction
to the Aristotelian prescription for creating great
art. (Incidentally, Harris's paper departs from the
balance of this volume in form as well as in con-

tent. Coming not only from theory but from experience, Harris's charming, informal address to the
conference works on the basis of practical insights
gleaned from a lifelong romance with the cinema and
his recent experiences as a screenwriter.)

In filmmaking, according to Harris, it is
aesthetic "Accident" rather than "Necessity and
Probability" that is often the energizing factor.
The film is shaped, finally, not by a creative
artist manipulating structure to create meaning but
by an all-powerful producer whose awesome "final
cut" manipulates film "properties" to create profits. It would be hard to conceive two more anti-
thetical or antipodal descriptions of the artistic
process than Aristotle's theory of artistic excellence and Harris's description of the realities of
filmmaking. Harris tells us that when a classic or
memorable film is made those who have made it will
not know how they did it and will not be able to
establish the conditions for making it again. The
"flying elephants" in the title of his paper illustrate his point very well. They had been created
for some long-forgotten purpose and were inserted
for no apparent artistic reason in a Laurel and
Hardy film. He suggests that they were lying
around the studio and someone decided to make some
use at last of an earlier investment. Harris does
not think that the average movie producer spends
much time worrying about necessity, probability,
and cathartic illumination. Instead, he has a
profit to make and resources to use, and these
determine what will happen in a film. The things
that meant so much to Aristotle, described in
Harris's words as "theme, meaning, point, purpose,
moral intention, political viewpoint, ethical outlook or philosophy," are "irrelevant to the will of
the producer seeking the element, the bankable certainty, the customer's desire."

The issue between Aristotle's prescription for
the creation of the best tragedy and Harris's description of the creation of most films is the tension between aesthetic control exercised by a poet's
vision and the arbitrary decisions made by a producer in search of commercial success. The two ap-
proaches intersect very rarely when the search for a
box office smash hit stumbles miraculously onto
cathartic illumination.

2

WOMEN NOVELISTS AND THE MALE-FEMALE

DOUBLE BILDUNGSROMAN

Charlotte Goodman

Although the Bildungsroman has been a genre of
longstanding interest to literary scholars, only
recently have critics begun to draw distinctions
between Bildungsromane written by men and Bildungsromane written by women[1]--or indeed, to give any
sustained attention to Bildungsromane written by
women. Certainly, in discussing the evolution of
the Bildungsroman as a genre, critics frequently
refer to a few selected works by women, among them,
perhaps, Charlotte Brontë's Jane Eyre or George
Eliot's The Mill on the Floss. However, usually
beginning with an examination of Goethe's Wilhelm
Meister, the majority of studies of the Bildungsroman not only focus almost entirely on novels
written by males about male protagonists, but also
define the genre in terms that apply almost exclusively to male experience.[2]
In this paper I shall describe briefly a group
of Bildungsromane written by women novelists, including Emily Brontë's Wuthering Heights (1847),
George Eliot's The Mill on the Floss (1860), Willa
Cather's My Antonia (1918), Jean Stafford's The
Mountain Lion (1947), and Joyce Carol Oates's them
(1969). While these works incorporate many of the
generic features of the typical Bildungsroman, they
also depart from this male-defined genre in signif-

icant ways: instead of tracing the growth and development of a single protagonist, as the prototypical
Bildungsroman does, these Bildungsromane by women
novelists describe the evolution of a pair of protagonists, one male and one female. Tripartite in
structure, such double Bildungsromane first depict
the shared childhood experience of a boy and a girl
who inhabit a prelapsarian garden world in which the
male and the female child exist as equals; then
dramatize the separation of the male and the female
characters in adolescence and young adulthood as the
male, like the hero of the typical male Bildungsroman, journeys forth to seek his fortune while the
female remains behind; and finally, conclude with a
reunion of the male and female protagonists. While
the structure of the typical male Bildungsroman is
linear, beginning in childhood and progressing towards the moment when the mature male adult, having
cast off the restraints of his earlier life, faces
the future, the structure of the male-female double
Bildungsroman is circular, concluding with the return of the male protagonist to seek his female
counterpart. This return, I believe, signifies a
turning away from mature adult experience and a
retrogression to the golden childhood world in which
the male and female protagonists were undivided. I
would argue that this double form of the Bildungsroman is particularly congenial to the woman novelist who wishes to emphasize the constraints that a
patriarchal society imposes on women. The inter-
dependence of the male and female protagonists un a
psychological as well as a narrative level strongly
suggests that each character represents a part of a
single, androgynous individual, the male and the
female characters in such novels appearing to function as psychological "doubles," each intensely involved in the psychic life of his or her counterpart, and each representing a conflicting aspect of
the author's own psychic life. Looked at together,
the male and the female characters suggest androgynous wholeness, a state imaginable only in a prelapsarian childhood world before sexual differentiation occurs. Offering a critique of a society in
which gender roles are rigidly assigned, the male-
female double Bildungsroman, then, traces the way in
which a harmonious and balanced androgynous self is
split asunder by a world which insists that adult

males and females play radically different roles.
Only in the final scene of each novel is the divi-
sion between the male and the female self healed
momentarily.

The prototype for the male-female double Bildungsroman was established in the nineteenth century
by Emily Brontë in Wuthering Heights and by George
Eliot in The Mill on the Floss. In both novels, an
assertive, energetic young girl spends her most
pleasurable moments in childhood with a boy companion, but is separated from him in early adolescence.
Brontë describes the early lives of Catherine
Earnshaw and Heathcliff as idyllic, for in the outdoor world of the moors that they roam together, the
female young lady of the manor and the foundling
"gypsy brat,"[3] free from the constraints of conventional society, are able to exist as equals. George
Eliot's protagonists, Maggie and Tom Tulliver, too,
inhabit an Edenic garden world in early childhood,
until they pass through the "golden gates" in early
adolescence.[4] All too soon, however, the male and
female of the pairs in each of these novels are
separated: while the first parts of these novels
emphasize the shared experience of their respective
male and female protagonists, the middle and major
portions of the narratives describe the social
forces that bring about the characters' separation
as they begin to assume their divergent adult roles.
Thus, Brontë's Catherine is transformed from a bare-
foot, wild, androgynous child into a ladylike person
who is afraid to soil her fingers, now "wonderfully
whitened with doing nothing and staying indoors,"
by shaking hands with the grimy Heathcliff.[5] Once
Catherine is groomed to take her place as the gen-
teel wife of the proper Edgar Linton, her "Bildung"
or education is over. Her married life is depicted
in terms of entrapment, progressive mental derange-
ment, and increasing physical disability, until she
dies in childbirth, as did so many women of Brontë's
day. Eliot's adolescent Maggie Tulliver, too, is
depicted as being confined and restricted by the new
demands of adult life. No longer permitted to be a
tomboy, she is forced to spend her time indoors
helping with the housework or sewing, chores she
loathed as a child. In contrast to Catherine and
Maggie, however, Heathcliff and Tom Tulliver move
out into the greater world: Heathcliff sets forth

on the typical journey of the Bildungsroman hero
from country to city to make his fortune, and Tom
Tulliver leaves home, first to receive the education
of a gentleman and later to redeem his family's for-
tunes.

Whereas the typical Bildungsroman ends with the
male protagonist facing a future of enlarged possibilities, the novels of Brontë and Eliot do not conclude until their respective male and female protagonists are reunited. Brontë's and Eliot's novels
both suggest that until such reconciliation takes
place, the male and the female characters are each
incomplete, and both authors emphasize the depriva-
tion that the female character, in particular, suffers because of her limited options. The oft-quoted
line in which Catherine exclaims about Heathcliff,
"He's more myself than I am. Whatever our souls are
made of, his and mine are the same,"[6] suggests that
Brontë wishes us to view her two characters as in-
tegral parts of a single being. Separated in life
by their divergent social roles, the protagonists
of Wuthering Heights are reunited only when
Heathcliff dies, years after Catherine, exulting in
the knowledge that in death he and Catherine will be
rejoined. Like Catherine and Heathcliff, Maggie and
Tom Tulliver also are united only in death. At the
end of The Mill on the Floss, Eliot tells us that
Maggie and Tom, who drown in a flood, are finally
able to return to the golden days of their childhood
when "they had clasped their little hands in love
and roamed the daisy fields together."[7] Maudlin
though it may be, this passage succeeds in evoking
the evanescent harmony of a prelapsarian world where
the male-female self was undivided.

Three twentieth-century novels by women that also
employ the basic pattern of the male-female double
Bildungsroman are Willa Cather's My Antonia, Jean
Stafford's The Mountain Lion, and Joyce Carol
Oates's them. In each we find a double protagonist
as well as the tripartite structure that is employed
so effectively by Emily Brontë and George Eliot.
Though they differ in concrete detail, My Antonia,
The Mountain Lion, and them, like Wuthering Heights
and The Mill on the Floss, appear to originate in a
mythical world where male and female are undivided.
Through their binary structure they dramatize the
tragic fragmentation that growing up entails, es-

pecially for girls whose culture insists that they
conform to narrowly defined female roles, while
their male counterparts are free to journey into the
world.

In Cather's My Antonia, as in the earlier novels
I have discussed, childhood, set in a rural outdoor
environment, is described as an idyllic period in
the life of the two protagonists, Jim Burden, the
narrator of the novel, and Antonia Shimerda, a
Bohemian immigrant girl. Though Jim is four years
younger than she, Jim and Antonia function as equals
during their childhood, exploring the Nebraska
countryside together. Very quickly, however, Cather
shows this Edenic period coming to a close as Jim
goes to school in town and later to the university
to prepare for a career as a lawyer, while Antonia
remains at home in the provincial town of Black
Hawk. Seduced and then abandoned by a lover,
Antonia goes through a period of great unhappiness
during which she bears a child out of wedlock, but
later she builds a more satisfying life as the wife
of a Bohemian farmer and mother of a large family.
My Antonia concludes with a scene of reconciliation
between the male and the female protagonists. Although Jim, unhappily married and childless, sees
Antonia's life as more fulfilling than his own,
Cather suggests that a vital part of Antonia has
perforce been sacrificed as she assumes her adult
female role, for despite the fact that she is proud
of her accomplishments as a wife and mother, she
tells Jim that she wishes a better life for her own
daughter than the confining life she herself has
been obliged to lead. "I'm going to see that my
little girl has a better chance than I ever had,"
she informs him.[8] Though critics have often viewed
this novel as celebrating the "heart," represented
by Antonia, over the "head," represented by Jim,[9] I
believe that Cather's vision is at once more complex
and more ambiguous: through her use of a double protagonist, she articulates her tragic sense that in a
male-dominated culture, a single individual cannot
experience both the maternal fulfillment of an
Antonia and the intellectual fulfillment of a Jim
Burden. When Cather has Jim say to Antonia, "The
idea of you is part of my mind. . . . You really are
a part of me," Cather appears to be suggesting that
each represents a part of a single, divided

psyche.[10]   The gulf between Jim's experience and
that of Antonia is bridged only by Jim's imagination
and Cather's art.

The two most recent examples of the male-female
double Bildungsroman, which I shall describe briefly, are Jean Stafford's The Mountain Lion and Joyce
Carol Oates's them. Focusing on a brother and sister, both of these Bildungsromane once again present contrasting images of male and female experience, as Stafford and Oates, respectively, trace
the early bonding of their protagonists, their subsequent separation in adolescence, and their final
reunion. While the male protagonists of Stafford
and Oates, like those of Brontë, Eliot, and Cather,
are depicted as independent and self-actualizing,
their female protagonists are shown to be insecure
and depressive. During adolescence Stafford's
Ralph Fawcett and Oates's Jules Wendall leave behind
the childhood world they have shared with their sisters, take on new roles, and are initiated into
adult sexuality. Their female counterparts, however, become increasingly morose when confronted
with the limited and limiting options that life
offers to them. Whereas sexuality represents ex-
panding possibilities to the male characters, each
female character comes to view sexual experience as
a form of entrapment: Molly Fawcett, who dreams of
being a writer like Mark Twain, is embarrassed by
her body and prefers to think of herself as "a long
wooden box with a mind inside,"[11] and Oates's
Maureen Wendall fears that she will end up as an
overburdened working-class housewife like her
mother. While the images that Stafford and Oates
use to describe Ralph and Jules are images of movement and change, they describe their female protagonists in terms of images of stasis and confinement:
retreating more and more into herself, Stafford's
Molly imagines locking herself in a bathroom and
living there alone until she dies; and Maureen
Wendall withdraws into a catatonic stupor after she
is brutally assaulted by her stepfather. Parallel-
ing the other male-female Bildungsromane I have discussed in this paper, Stafford's The Mountain Lion
and Oates's them both conclude with a final scene in
which the male and female protagonists, separated in
adolescence, are brought together once again. The
ending of Stafford's novel is more tragic than that

of any of the other novels since it is Ralph
Fawcett, who embodies all the attitudes of the
patriarchal male, that directly causes the destruc-
tion of his sister when he accidentally shoots her
instead of a female mountain lion he had set out to
kill.

The underlying structure of union, separation,
and return, which I have identified as characteristic of the male-female double Bildungsromane discussed in this paper, emphasizes the dichotomy between male and female experience in a patriarchal
culture. By introducing a modification into the
traditional structure of the Bildungsroman, Brontë,
Eliot, Cather, Stafford, and Oates are able to contrast the traditional "education" of males and females. In childhood, the male and the female are
unusually close. In adolescence, however, when
sexual differentiation occurs, the male journeys
forth, as does the typical hero of the single
Bildungsroman, while the female protagonist either
remains close to home or in an enclosed environment.
The conclusion of the male-female double Bildungsroman differs most significantly from that of the
traditional Bildungsroman, for instead of contem-
plating the future, as do the protagonists of the
latter, the male protagonist of the male-female
double Bildungsroman returns to the world of his
childhood to embrace his female counterpart, allowing the male and the female halves of the divided
self to be reunited once again. As male and female
confront one another at the end of each of these
novels, the reader is made aware of the radically
different kinds of "education" each has undergone.
Only in the final meeting that occurs is the divi-
sion of the androgynous self, as projected through
the binary structure of the double Bildungsroman,
healed through the alchemy of the author's art.

NOTES

[1]See for example Annis Pratt, "The New Feminist
Criticism," College English 32 (1970-71): 877.

[2]See Jerome Buckley, Season of Youth: The Bildungsroman from Dickens to Golding (Cambridge: Harvard University Press, 1974).

[3]Emily Brontë, Wuthering Heights, ed. William M. Sale, Jr. (New York: Norton Critical Editions, 1972), p. 39.

[4]George Eliot, The Mill on the Floss, bk. 2, chap. 7.

[5]Brontë, p. 51.

[6]Brontë, p. 72.

[7]Eliot, bk. 7, chap. 5.

[8]Willa Cather, My Antonia (Boston: Houghton Mifflin, 1954), p. 320.

[9]See for example John H. Randall III, The Landscape and the Looking Glass: Willa Cather's Search for Value (Boston: Houghton Mifflin, 1960), pp. 106-108.

[10]Cather, p. 321.

[11]Jean Stafford, The Mountain Lion (New York: Farrar, Strauss, and Giroux, 1972), p. 177.

3

"EVERYTHING AND NOTHING": THE MYTH OF PERSONAL

IDENTITY IN JORGE LUIS BORGES

AND BERGMAN'S PERSONA

Maurice J. Bennett

This essay is an inquiry into the emotional, psychological, and spiritual values that our civilization provides for the valorization of individual existence. As great artists, Bergman and Borges are important indices of its notion of significant being. Bergman represents the culmination of a tradition that began with the Romantics and now finds its definitive expression in the revolutionary medium of film. Borges, however, is the inaugurator of a literary tradition that is progressively moving toward a central position in contemporary letters.[1] Both represent the West; but where in one there is the luminosity of a kind of decadence, in the other there is the elan of what, perhaps, marks a new beginning.

The Mexican poet and intellectual Octavio Paz writes that analogy and irony are the dominant modes of Romantic and post-Romantic art, and that both result from the Romantics' protest against the linear time of history.[2] Analogy conflates past and future into the present, transforms Earth into a reflection of Heaven, and considers the universe a text, the exegesis of which is the salvation of man. Irony, however, "shows that if the universe is a

17

script, each translation of this script is different, and that the concert of correspondences is the
gibberish of Babel. The poetic word ends in a howl
or in silence: irony is not a word, nor a speech,
but a reverse of the word, noncommunication." The
sudden muteness of the actress Elizabeth Vogler and
the progressive collapse of her young nurse, Alma,
into the inarticulate, point to Bergman's choice of
the ironic key in Persona, his commitment to an
"aesthetics of the grotesque, the bizarre and the
unique." However, the syncretism and mythologies,
the alchemical and magical transformations that
form the substance of Borges's work represent his
preference for analogy, for the "aesthetics of
correspondences." It is in terms of this contrast
between the unique and the archetypal, the individual and the metapersonal, that the "self" dramatized
by these two artists assumes its disparate configu-
rations.

One of the most important images in Persona is
that in which the faces of the two women are combined into a single visage. Bergman thus emphasizes
the theme of doubling that places the film squarely
within a literary tradition that has expressed man's
concern with the failure of psychic unity through
its preoccupation with twins, doubles, and second
selves. He recapitulates and exhausts the themes
and techniques of this literature, so that there is
both the issue of a kind of psycho-emotional vampir-
ism between two distinct characters and that of a
conflict between two halves of a single psyche.[3]

Alma's ceaseless chatter, her apparent devotion
to nonpurposive speech, makes her a naive version of
Elizabeth: either currently or in the immediate past
both women exist for an audience as language. But
it is Elizabeth's dilemma that is the film's donnée;
her action (or inaction) and her silence make Alma
possible by creating the need for her. Thus, as far
as the narrative is concerned, Alma is born from
Elizabeth's speechlessness. "If only because the
artwork exists in a world furnished with many other
things," observes Susan Sontag, "the artist who
creates silence or emptiness must produce something
dialectical: a full void, an enriching emptiness, a
resonating or eloquent silence."[4] Here, the artistic problem is solved by Alma's loquacity. The
speech that Elizabeth, the artist, rejects

is projected onto her naive soul, where it undergoes
the appropriate transformation. Since Elizabeth
cannot cease speaking altogether, she interiorizes
language, so that Alma, as the second self, becomes
a kind of externalization of internal soliloquy.

There remains, however, the discrepancy between
the naive, unreflective patter that Alma casts into
the void of Elizabeth's silence and the more complex
discourses her patient-double has relinquished. In
a sense, Elizabeth's offscreen seizure by silence
results in a restoration of whatever has been rejected or repressed. As an artist, an actress
existing primarily in a series of autonomous and
disconnected "roles," she had no self; her identity
was subordinated to the script, an alien text, and
thus represented the latest version of Keats's
notion of the artist's "negative capability." "As
to the poetical Character itself," he wrote in a
letter to Richard Woodhouse, "it is not itself--it
has no self--it is every thing and nothing--It has
no character. . . ."[5] Her willful grasp of neuro-
sis, then, is a negation that leads to a restitu-
tion: the self that she had either repressed or
banished reappears before her. She has annulled
her relationship to others, to an audience, in order
to be reduced to a single relationship--that with
herself. Thus, her withdrawal to the beach house
duplicates the hallowed strategy of certain Romantic
protagonists--Werther and René, for instance; it
protects from external scrutiny and evaluation her
newly rediscovered and possessed subjectivity.[6]

One critic claims that the image of the composite
face mentioned earlier is "a sick, monstrous face
that does not hang together--that contradicts itself, wants to split apart, is struggling against an
enforced oneness," and he interprets it as a symbol
of the struggle between the artist and the common
man.[7] However, more consistent with the details of
the film and the intellectual climate it consciously
imports is a notion of the traditional Romantic
internalization of this struggle. The psychological
problem is the artist's relationship to himself; the
moral issue is the relationship of intellect and
imagination to those common human emotions that
nourish them and that are shared with other men; and
the ontological consideration involves the relationship of the aesthetic self to the naive self it once

was and, in a sense, continues to be. Alma's suffering, then, is the inevitable writhing to which
the aesthetic self reduces the more conventional
self trapped in the same body; it is in the best
tradition of Hoffmann, Mary Shelley, and Stevenson.

Elizabeth's silence inevitably raises the question of the search for authenticity. Her psychia-
trist offers this as a possible explanation of her
behavior, and, despite the complexity of subsequent
confrontations and evasions, it projects into the
narrative one of the major issues of twentieth-
century aesthetic and philosophical discourse: the
interrogation of the validity of language as an
instrument and sign of being. In her "The Aesthetics of Silence," Sontag identifies a tendency
among contemporary artists to strive for a tran-
scendence of the masteries and solaces of their art,
and Emile Cioran, himself a frustrated apostle of
silence and stillness, asserts that salvation de-
pends on man's "debaptizing the universe, by remov-
ing the labels which, assigned to each appearance,
isolates it and lends it a simulacrum of meaning."8
With regard to gesture, he writes that "Every act
institutes and rehabilitates plurality, and, con-
ferring reality and autonomy upon the person, im-
plicitly recognizes the degradation and parceling-
out of the absolute," and he urges that "the only
free mind is one that, pure of all intimacy with
beings and objects, plies its own vacuity."

As the gesture of a latter-day artist,
Elizabeth's behavior inhabits a context of similar
considerations, both because they are admirably
suited to render it intelligible and, more simply
and incontrovertibly, because Bergman himself inten-
tionally raises the issue through the doctor.
Elizabeth's metaphorical stillness (her retirement
from acting) and her literal muteness occupy the
same aesthetic terrain as the efforts of a Mallarmé
or a Robbe-Grillet to abolish or transcend the
vagaries of the Word.

This preoccupation with authentic speech is in-
separable from the question of authentic selfhood.
At one point, Alma herself offers a theory of language and being, questioning whether speech and life
need be truthful. "Isn't it better to be silly,
lax, babbling and lying?" she asks. "Don't you
think one improves a little even by letting oneself

be as one is?" This is precisely the experiment
that Elizabeth has undertaken: her silence effectively questions both the languages and the selves
of her former existence by abruptly halting their
endless proliferation. But her stillness and her
silence constitute a peculiar beatitude. On one
level, they generate Alma's monologue, but on another, they become a compulsion, a violence, an
aggression directed at the nurse's speech; they
surround, highlight, and eventually absorb it,
thereby threatening her ontological distinctness.[9]

In the film's tortured encounters, Elizabeth is
frightened into screaming, once; from her bright
certainties, Alma is reduced to sobs and disconnected exclamations. Elizabeth's silence erodes
Alma's speech until both women exist on analogous
levels of noncommunication. Which, then, is the
more authentic self: Elizabeth with her silence and
abnegation, or Alma with her naive complacencies?
The stylized, aesthetic discourse of art is rejected
for silence; the evasive, cliché-ridden speech of
every day ends in gibberish. The possibilities of
meaning and of significant selfhood are thus undermined by a universal criticism that mocks all per-
spectives.

Against the kind of bleakness envisioned by
Bergman's corrosive, triumphant irony, however,
Borges constructs an affirmation. The Word retains
its original divine efficacy, and language, far from
being the instrument of man's detachment from being
--the agent of his pain and despair--becomes the
means by which he eternally recreates himself and
the universe. "Every cultivated man is a theolo-
gian," he writes, while admitting his own "incredu-
lous and persistent enthusiasm for theological difficulties" (OI,76;D,9).[10] Thus, epiphany and apotheosis are the characteristic events of his tales,
as he attempts an escape from the linear time of
Augustinian Christianity and modern history and a
corollary liberation from the unique, isolated self
they imply. He condemns modern literature, with its
"shapeless psychological writing" (A,274), and modern philosophy as "immoral" because, "although they
may play at desperation and anguish," they "foster
the illusion of the self" and thereby "flatter the
vanity" (OI,166). And he notes "the insupportable
and tragic solitude of the person who lacks a place,

even a most humble one, in the order of the universe" (OI,34).

In order to create that place, he turns to the
doctrines of the East and to the heresies and eso-
terica of the West. The central myth that under-
lies his tales is adumbrated in the myth of the
Simurg; his reiterated image of the universe is the
Aleph. In the former, the birds, searching for
their king, pass through a series of trials only to
discover that they are each the monarch they have
sought. Not only is divinity parcelled among multi-
tudes, but the extinction of purely individual being
is indicated by the nature of the obstacles separating the birds from their king's Holy Mountain: the
mountains "Vertigo" and "Annihilation."

Appended to what Borges considers his paradig-
matic tale, "The Approach to al-Mu'tasim," the myth
of the Simurg operates as a reiteration and an
interpretation. "The Approach" takes the form of a
review of a fictional novel by one Mir Bahadur Ali
whose theme is "the untiring search for a human soul
through the barely perceptible reflections cast by
this soul in others" (A,49). Al-Mu'tasim, "he of
the unimaginable voice," the shining light behind
the curtain, is the object of the protagonist's
search, and the reviewer paraphrases: "The nearer
to al-Mu'tasim the men he examines are, the greater
is their share of the divine, though it is under-
stood that they are but mirrors" (A,49). Usually
in the literature of the multiple self, the mirror
image demonstrates to the perceiving self its validity; but, in Borges, mirrors connect the self not
with its literal reflection, but with its divine
archetype. More than the instruments of an affirmative doubling, mirrors ceaselessly replicate the
divine image itself. Thus, Borges affirms the
denial of the existence of the self by the Vedas
and by Schopenhauer, who posit merely a succession
of observers, each the mirror image of the other
(OI,19).

Such doctrines ignore notions of concrete, linear, irreversible time--History--and create what
Mircea Eliade calls "archaic ontology," in which
objects and human acts "become real, because they
participate . . . in a reality that transcends
them." Primitive or "archaic" man "acknowledges no
act which has not been previously posited and lived

by someone else, some other being who was not a
man."[11] Like the birds in search of the Simurg, the
protagonist of "The Approach" is seeking God, who is
also himself. More significantly, his search duplicates a divine action with which it becomes identi-
cal through repetition. Al-Mu'tasim, the reviewer
observes, etymologically means "The Seeker After
Help," and he suggests that "the Almighty is also in
search of Someone, and that Someone of Someone above
him . . . and so on to the End (or rather, Endless-
ness) of Time, or perhaps cyclically" (A,50). The
human quest for identity thus achieves meaning by
participating in an archetypal cosmic event; it is
the quest for an identity that is not located in
time but situated at the end of an eternal regres-
sion, or ascension, to original divinity.
    Where the myth of the Simurg establishes the
Unity of the individual with all others and with
the divine, the Aleph posits the radical unity of
the universe. It is the first letter of the Hebrew
alphabet and the cabalistic symbol of absolute divinity. Pictorially represented as a man pointing
at both Heaven and Earth, it is also a symbol of
their correspondence, the triumph of Analogy. Thus,
the protagonist of the story, "The Aleph," achieves
this epiphany: "I saw a small iridescent sphere of
almost unbearable brilliance. At first I thought it
was revolving; then I realized that this movement
was an illusion created by the dizzying world it
bounded. . . . all space was there, actual and un-
diminished. Each thing (a mirror's face, let us
say) was infinite things, since I distinctly saw it
from every angle of the universe. . . . I felt dizzy
and wept, for my eyes had seen that secret and con-
jectured object whose name is common to all men but
which no man has looked upon--the unimaginable universe" (A,26-28). Borges repeatedly returns to this
vision of multiplicity and unity, coexistent and
mutually implicated--whether as the magical coin,
the zahir, Pascal's "infinite sphere having its
center everywhere and its circumference nowhere," or
the circle of fire and water dreamed by the protagonist of "The Handwriting of God."
    For Eliade's "archaic man," an object becomes
sacred "and hence instantly becomes saturated with
being--because it represents a hierophany, possesses
mana"; it is "incomprehensible, invulnerable" be-

cause it "resists time; its reality is coupled with
perenniality."[12] The Aleph, then, represents the
value of each fact and each moment as revelation.
It is another version of Borges's assertion that
"the smallest facts presuppose the inconceivable
universe, and, inversely . . . the universe, needs
the least of its facts" (D,11).

If all fact is a potential Aleph and all men are
God, then all men are also all things, and the
privileged exemplar of this state of multiple being,
historically, has been the artist. Always in
Borges, the poet is obligated to exhaust the possibilities of being, to include the abysms as well as
the exaltations of human nature. The Icelandic poet
Ulf Sigurdsson, in search of the single word that
comprises the poetry of the Urns--a verbal Aleph--
must first undergo a series of adventures that makes
him "an oarsman, slave dealer, slave, highwayman,
singer, and taster of deep waters and metals." And
he confesses that "In the course of time I have been
many men; it was a whirlwind, a long dream, but all
the while the main thing was the Word" (S,85,86).
Of course, it is Shakespeare, since the Romantics
exalted him as the archetypal poet, whose portrait
furnishes this essay with a title, "Everything and
Nothing." Borges thus imagines the climactic scene
of his career:

> History adds that before or after his death
> he found himself facing God and said: I, who
> have been so many men in vain, want to be one
> man, myself alone. From out of a whirlwind
> the voice of God replied: I am not, either. I
> dreamed the world the way you dreamed your
> work, my Shakespeare: one of the forms of my
> dream was you, who, like me, are many and no
> one. (PA,116-117)

The loss of self and the multiplication of identity
in the artwork, thus, are modelled after the original act of creation, and the artist once more appears as the avatar of God.

As the self-appointed diagnosticians of the
senescence of a civilization, Western artists and
intellectuals have lamented not only the collapse of
those philosophical and religious systems that
charged individual acts and individual being with

significance, but also the atrophy of the very capa-
city for _collective_ vision. For instance, Sontag
charges that, intellectually, Western man has been
reduced to a doctrine of every man for himself,
"_sauve qui peut_"--the ethics of defeat and isolation.[13] "Modern philosophy, by establishing the
superstition of the Ego, has made it the mainspring
of our dramas and the pivot of our anxieties,"
writes Emile Cioran; "we have chosen to be _subjects_,
and every subject is a break with the quietude of
Unity."[14] _Persona_ originates in this "superstition
of the Ego"; it assumes the ontological validity of
the self by advancing the legitimacy, the actuality,
of its suffering. Personality constitutes a problematic here, which presupposes a belief in--or, at
least, a nostalgia for--the rationalist conception
of a unified self existing in time. The film
finally represents the culmination of a modern
tradition translated into the latest artistic genre,
embellished and exhausted by the resources of the
cinema. Whether described as an encounter between
two women or as the confrontation between a single
figure and herself, the action is entirely decon-
textualized, except for the intellectual-literary
tradition of self-scrutiny. Appealing to no values
or systems beyond those of the individual psychology, it becomes an anatomy of solipsism.

   In Borges, however, the _Fall_ into multiplicity--
although it inevitably involves degradation, pain,
and death--has as its final goal the recovery of
the Self beneath (or beyond) the agitations of the
ego. It therefore becomes an affirmative act that
repeats the original multiplication of Unity that
constituted the world. Bergman has claimed that
"The reality we experience today is in fact as
absurd, as horrible, and as obtrusive as our
dreams."[15] In a similar vein, Borges writes that
"the tumultuous general catastrophes--fires, wars,
epidemics--are but a single sorrow illusorily multi-
plied in many mirrors" (OI,178). However, where
Bergman implies a psychology of individuals isolated in a private terror, as divergent, personal,
and unique as their dreams, Borges indicates a meta-
reality of which personal experience is but a
reflection. Man can penetrate to this transpersonal
realm if he only has the courage to possess those

very dreams that are for Bergman the ingress of the horrible.

Borges's message is a consolation, and he writes: "In times of growth the conjecture that the existence of man is a constant, invariable quantity can sadden or irritate us; in times of general decline (like these), it is the promise that no opprobrium, no calamity, no dictator can impoverish us" (E,103). With this doctrine of personal and cosmic plenitude, he is the founder of a tradition in Latin American letters that has made it, at present, the world's most exciting body of literature. Cioran sees in the as of yet historically and culturally silent extensions of Europe (Latin America, Australia, South Africa) the possibility of life-giving infusions--the ever-declining West may be saved, not from the metropolitan center, but from "the suburbs of the globe."[16]

NOTES

[1]For notations of Borges's seminal role in the movement that has produced such internationally recognized figures as Márquez, Asturias, or Cortázar, see Angel Flores, "Magical Realism in Spanish American Fiction," Hispania 38 (May, 1955); 187-192; Carlos Fuentes, La nueva novela hispano-americana (Mexico City: Joaquin Mortiz, 1974), pp. 25-26, 68; and Octavio Paz, Children of the Mire: Modern Poetry from Romanticism to the Avant-Garde, trans. Rachel Phillips (Cambridge, Mass.: Harvard University Press, 1974), pp. 138-146.

[2]Paz, Children of the Mire. See particularly pages 58-77; all direct quotations are taken from pages 74 and 110.

[3]The simultaneous identity and distinction of the two characters; the mutual preoccupation that surfaces as a kind of sexual interest; the confusion between dream and objective fact; the presence of a character whose consciousness is revealed and shared and one who remains an enigma; and the opposition between the naive and the sinister are but a few of

the elements in the literary tradition that Bergman is exploiting here. See Carl F. Keppler, The Literature of the Second Self (Tucson, Arizona: The University of Arizona Press, 1972).

[4] Susan Sontag, "The Aesthetics of Silence," Styles of Radical Will (New York: Farrar, Straus and Giroux, 1966), p. 11.

[5] John Keats, The Poetical Works and Other Writings of John Keats, ed. H. Buxton Forman (New York: Phaeton Press, 1970), vol. 7, p. 129.

[6] For the outline of this argument, I am indebted to Irving Massey, The Un-Creating Word: Romanticism and the Object (Bloomington, Ind.: Indiana University Press, 1970), p. 49, and his The Gaping Pig: Literature and Metamorphosis (Berkeley, Ca.: University of California Press, 1976), p. 134.

[7] John Simon, Ingmar Bergman Directs (New York: Harcourt, Brace, Jovanovich, 1972), pp. 298, 304.

[8] Sontag, Radical Will, pp. 6-7. All other quotations in this paragraph are from Emile Cioran, "Thinking Against Oneself," The Temptation to Exist, trans. Richard Howard (Chicago: Quadrangle Books, 1968), pp. 46, 42, 39.

[9] See Tzvetan Todorov's discussion of the pre- and post-linguistic worlds of the child, the drug user, and the mystic--their silence--as a virtual obliteration of the subject-object split in his The Fantastic: A Structural Approach to a Literary Genre, trans. Richard Howard (Cleveland: The Press of Case Western Reserve University, 1973), pp. 145-146.

[10] All citations from Borges's work will be included in the text as an abbreviation and a page number: A, The Aleph and Other Stories, 1933-1969, trans. Norman Thomas di Giovanni (New York: E. P. Dutton, 1970); OI, Other Inquisitions, 1937-1952, trans. Ruth L. Syms (New York: Simon and Schuster, 1964); PA, A Personal Anthology (New York: Grove Press, 1967); S, The Book of Sand, trans. Norman Thomas di Giovanni (New York: E. P. Dutton, 1978). Translations from the following are my own: D, Discusion, (Buenos Aires: Emece Editores, 1957);

E, _Historia de la Eternidad_ (Buenos Aires: Emece Editores, 1971).

[11]Mircea Eliade, _The Myth of the Eternal Return, or, Cosmos and History_, trans. Willard R. Trask (Princeton: Princeton University Press, 1965), pp. 4, 5.

[12]Ibid., p. 4.

[13]Sontag, _Radical Will_, p. 75.

[14]Cioran, _Temptation_, p. 43.

[15]From an interview quoted in John Simon, _Ingmar Bergman Directs_, p. 239.

[16]Cioran, p. 64.

4

THE DYNAMICS OF TARDIEU'S

LE MEUBLE

Sylvie Debevec Henning

At first sight, Le Meuble, a one-act playlet
written by Jean Tardieu in the early fifties, appears extremely bewildering. It presents to us, as
spectators or readers, an unstable object, or rather
an unsettling subject: the "mechanical protagonist,"
le meuble, more an animated invention than a piece
of furniture. Our problem then becomes one of interpretation. What are we to do with Tardieu's
Meuble in this double sense, that is, either as the
play itself or as the contraption from which it
takes its name?
We shall begin by considering them both as examples of a particular kind of work of art--the grotesque. What we have before us, in other words,
could be construed as a grotesque "object" within a
grotesque play. This study does not mean to suggest, as have some contemporary discussions, that
the grotesque play is merely the grotesque object
set in motion.[1] Rather, it hopes to demonstrate

This essay first appeared as part of "Le Meuble:
Tardieu's Grotesque Con-trap-tion" in Stanford
French Review, 6(1) and is reproduced here by per-
mission of the publisher, Anma Libri.

that both the grotesque object and the grotesque
play are, each within itself, equally constituted by
a network of dynamic relationships. As grotesques,
neither is static. Each develops over time and in a
similar way, viz., by exploiting that which is potentially unsettling in the traditionally comic as
well as what is latently uncanny in the all-too-
familiar. This "moving backwards," as it were, in
order to bring into play elements in the familiar
and the comic that are usually repressed or obscured, permits the grotesque to destabilize the
seemingly natural order.

Heteroclite and excessive, indeed comic like a
nonsense joke in its bizarre assemblage of incompatible elements, le meuble as contraption can, it
seems, truly be called a grotesque, for it clearly
transgresses the classical canons of aesthetics.
According to those rules, art is to be the truthful
representation of definite things, restricting itself to simple and perfected forms that have a basis
in nature, to things that really exist in the natural world or are historically accurate. Hard and
well-established lines are drawn between phenomena,
each seen as finished, completed, strictly limited,
and finding its place in an unchanging hierarchy.
Artistic principles, based on traditional Aristotelian logic, have been directly subverted by the
grotesque since at least the wall paintings in the
so-called Baths of Titus so scornfully described by
the Augustan theorist Vitruvius.[2] We find in these
early ornamental grotesques, first of all, an attack
on the principles of identity and difference. A
flower is not only a flower but also an animal; a
stem supports a blossom but also a roof. In addition, the static representation of reality has been
disturbed and with it the law of contradiction.
There are no longer finished forms--vegetable, animal, mineral--in a finished and stable world. Instead we find a more fluid and dynamic presentation
in which one form passes gradually into another.
Objects, phenomena, even situations, appear both as
themselves and as something else in order to suggest that they are already and always more than
themselves.

The ancestor of the Inventor's contraption appears to be a baroque descendant of these grotesques:

> Ce genre de meubles existe depuis fort
> longtemps, je n'hésite pas à le dire. Au
> XVIIIe siècle, on les appelait des "va-voir-
> si-j'y-suis." J'en ai vu de fort beaux, de
> cette époque-là: avec des pieds tournés en
> dedans, capsules de rechange, ambiance "Chez-
> soi" et cris de détresse en mer, le tout
> recouvert d'un damier, ébène et porphyre,
> muni de pédales en maroquin verni et agrémenté
> d'intervalles de séparation. . . .[3]

Looking at this portrait more closely, we find that
certain expressions, belonging to the decorator's
vocabulary, could actually be used to describe a
piece of furniture, although "capsules de rechange"
seems to announce murderous capabilities. Others,
however, like "pieds tournés en dedans" or "cris de
détresse en mer" may suggest instead human connotations. Inherently, then, this type of contraption
possesses at least the potential for disturbing the
traditional opposition between the animate and the
inanimate.
    We might even say that the unsettling quality of
the grotesque, particularly in its literary form,
may partially derive from the exploitation of certain potentially disturbing qualities of the language itself that creates it. In his discussion of
jokes, for example, Freud points to the intrinsi-
cally double nature of the witticism.[4] At first,
many witty expressions appear somewhat absurd or
foolish, as they overstep the restrictions of conventional word usage and logical arrangement. We
therefore find them pleasantly amusing. Freud suggests that this pleasure, which is a welcome relax-
ation of the psychically strenuous demands imposed
by rational discipline and order, finds its source
in the unconscious. These jokes, however, may also
disturb the conscious mind precisely because they
permit the uncanny return of this repressed irra-
tionalism. Consequently, the witty expression must
at least attempt to appease the conscious mind with
some sort of acceptable meaning. At the same time,
nonsense wit may be a vehicle for aggression. While
Freud tended to consider such verbal hostility as a
substitute for direct personal assault, its object
may be more general and its attack more significant.
It may, that is, be aimed at the entire system of

cultural norms, including those that regulate logical discourse.

The dialogue of Le Meuble is, in fact, largely
made up of such linguistic play. A small but telling example is the name of the meuble's baroque
predecessor, "va-voir-sij'y-suis." Seemingly foolish and nonsensical, it might be dismissed with a
chuckle. Yet, since it is really an idiomatic
expression used to dispose by trickery of somebody
unwanted, it is, at the same time, a trap for the
unsuspected, un piège-à-con. (Like a huckster, the
Inventor also refers to parts of his particular
meuble as "ni-vu-ni-connu" and "va-comme-je-te-
pousse," suggesting sleight of hand and manipula-
tion.) And it does, in fact, partially live up to
its name, almost succeeding to con the Buyer before
disposing of him. The absurd name, like the con-
trap-tion, is therefore indeed a booby trap.

It is not, however, only witticisms that contribute to the creation of grotesques. Language in general is potentially multiple insofar as ordinary
words contain within themselves a number of often
contradictory meanings. These can then be exploited
so as to make them seem at once familiarly comic and
dangerously uncanny. Le meuble, for example, is
described as a phenomenon: "Et voici le phenomène"
(p. 40). It is supposed, that is, to be something
that can be perceived and identified by the senses,
a piece of furniture, that is, a phenomenon in both
the ordinary and philosophical senses of the word.
Yet, in a secondary sense, a phenomenon is something
extraordinary, bizarre, or monstrous. And le meuble
is clearly that as well: "Que pensez-vois de cette
merveille?" (p. 42). The word "phenomenon," then,
signifies simultaneously the most commonplace thing
and the most rare; it is, like le meuble, already to
some degree at least potentially grotesque.

Not only does this polyvalence suggest that the
meanings of words are often contradictory or ambiguous, that is, not self-identical, but also that
they, like the Augustan grotesques, may cross categorial boundaries. The Inventor's contraption, for
example, is un meuble. In other words, it is by
definition "un object mobile." By exploiting its
etymology (mobile from the Latin mobilis, "qui se
meut"), we find that a mobile object, while generally considered one that can be moved, is, from a

certain perspective, also one with the ability to
move. The transition from inanimate invention to
animated protagonist is consequently already latent
in the word meuble itself.

The cross categorical confusion most important in
this particular meuble is precisely that between
inanimate and animate. We have already pointed to
those elements in the Inventor's description of its
baroque prototype that suggest human connotations.
The peculiar behavior of his own contraption seems
to develop out of implicit syllepses found in his
salesman's patter. An invention "sorti de [son]
cerveau et de [ses] mains," it was at its conception
more than an object, if not yet a person (p. 41).
He has put twenty-five years of his life, as well as
his youth and science, into this meuble. A banal
statement, it nonetheless opens the way for the investment of the machine with human attributes.
Moreover, the invention has "quelque chose dans le
ventre." In other words, it has guts, both literally and figuratively. And with such energy and
personality, it must have a soul (p. 41). Ein
Machinenmännchen, conceived in its creator's image,
it is, in addition, itself a pregnant creature about
to conceive. A truly metamorphous creature, it is
"plein à craquer," big with possibilities and highly
unstable.

A machine with such great powers might even become the arm of its Inventor. Having first been en-
dowed with human potentialities, it later acquires,
exploiting a resource buried in the description, a
humanoid appendage. Then, since it had earlier been
said to have a soul, it might even be filled with
spirit. With the logos comes speech: "Il est
parlant aussi, l'animal!" (p. 41). The animal en-
dowed with the faculty of discourse is evidently
here still a machine, but also somewhat of a man,
Descartes's distinction to the contrary. With the
ability to speak, it may also acquire a will of its
own. By going back once again to the initial description, in order to pick up and elaborate an
element that was left behind, we find that the trace
of this will was already potentially present in the
expression "avoir quelque chose dans le ventre,"
that is, "avoir de l'énergie et de la volonté." No
longer willing to obey its Inventor, le meuble is
dismissed like an overworked schoolboy. The Inven-

tor, explains that he has drilled too much of his
science too quickly into his pupil. But le meuble
has not, despite such schooling, lost his machinelike qualities, for its disturbances are said to
have both psychological and mechanical causes (p.
43). Overworked, insulted, punished, the machine
breaks down and, crac!, shoots and kills the Buyer.

We have seen how word witticism, in a broad
sense, contributes to the dynamic network of polysemous relations that constitute a grotesque "object" like le meuble. The manifold possibilities of
comedy, particularly as presented by Bergson, may be
similarly exploited. While le meuble, in its elaboration, appears to be retrieving its "inherited"
human traits, the Inventor seems to be reverting to
purely mechanical behavior. His speeches, like the
antique dealer's patter they parody, are made up of
worn-out clichés and stock hyperboles, repeated for
each customer with the slick assurance needed to
make him buy the product without thinking. It is to
this time-tested behavior that the Inventor returns
after the murder of his latest victim.

The mechanization of human activity, as exempli-
fied by the Inventor's behavior, may be related to
what Freud describes as a compulsion to repeat an
action, a compulsion that often strikes one as uncanny. In "Das Unheimliche," he explains that "the
principle of a repetition compulsion in the unconscious mind" is "based upon instinctual activities
and is probably inherent in the very nature of the
instincts."[5] He develops this further in Beyond
the Pleasure Principle where he adds that the most
primitive instinct is "the instinct to return to the
inanimate state."[6] By coming to resemble a machine,
then, the Inventor might be approaching what is in
fact the deathlike condition of static identity, one
which he would literally be essoufflé.

According to the theory Bergson put forth in Le
Rire, however, such machinelike repetition is the
essence of comedy: "du mécanique plaque sur du
vivant," "une certaine raideur du mécanique là où
l'on voudrait trouver la souplesse attentive et la
vivante flexibilité d'une personne."[7] The Inventor's propensity to repeat automatically may be
amusing, yet at the same time it is troubling, like
the music played on the barrel-organ at the beginning and end of the performance: "une musique

essoufflée d'orgue de Barbarie, une polka qui
voudrait être gaie mais qui, en fait, est déchirante
de tristesse, avec des notes qui manquent et des
halètements de mécanique usé" (p. 39). Like the
music, the Inventor is worn-out; he is essoufflé,
out of breath. He has lost his spirit and with it
his ability truly to create. Consequently, his
speeches and actions appear to be empty form, seemingly devoid of inspiration.

Bergson's redefinition of comedy can be related
to his criticism of the mechanistic interpretations
(among which could be included the mechanistic
models sometimes employed by Freud and subsequently
by certain Freudians) he believed did not allow for
the novelty and complexity necessary to continued
creative existence. The idea of a man-machine thus
appears comical to him because it is unnatural and
artificial. Bergson's own conception, however--
matter as the sphere of mechanism and spirit as that
of creative freedom--derives from and maintains the
same fundamental dualism as that upon which the
mechanists based their model. Consequently, it
tends to obscure the very complexity he seeks to
defend. Neither his vitalism nor the mechanism he
attacks appears adequately to address the issue of
the supplementary relations between the elements of
the dyad they posit.

In Beyond the Pleasure Principle, Freud also suggests that such repetition may be an attempt to
master, be reenacting it, a situation that origi-
nally caused tension or fright and was, for that
reason, repressed. But what could be the source of
the anxiety that the Inventor is trying to overcome
by repeating the same words and actions for each
customer? Perhaps it is le meuble itself, this contraption that refuses to remain in its own category.
By not obeying him, after all, it seems to render
problematic the neat oppositions on which his position is based: man/machine, inventor/invented, and
ultimately, spirit/matter. There is doubt, it appears, as to who is in fact calling the shot. It is
as if he hoped that, by trying long enough, he might
eventually force his contraption to conform to the
"natural" order. He turns the cause of his anxiety
into a form of play. By compulsively repeating the
actions that provoke his anxiety, the Inventor will
attempt to dominate it.

In summary, we might say that Le Meuble presents us with a grotesque reversal of roles: the contraption-like piece of furniture is metamorphosed into an anima-ted machine, while the uninspired Inventor comes to resemble an automaton. This study has suggested that this "development" is not strictly linear, for it "moves backwards" to exploit those remainders and traces of categorial ambiguities-- for example, the strange in the familiar, the unsettling in the comic, the animate in the inanimate, the mechanical in the human--that are still capable of being revived. By liberating, as it were, these repressed elements, it unsettles the classical conception of teleological evolution according to which things strive to embody as perfectly as may be their specific form. This conception implies, of course, that things have an essence or ideal identity, and that it is finally realizable. Le meuble, as we have seen, appears to be made up of a number of heteroclite elements that do not come together to form a perfect unity; indeed it does not even seem that it necessarily and logically had to end up as it did.

The force at work in the creation of le meuble as a grotesque monster may also be said to be at work within the elaboration of the play that parallels that creation. The time of the incomplete metamorphosis of the contraption into willful creature and the accompanying change in the Inventor is, after all, that of the play itself. And in its overall elaboration, no less than in that of its protagonist, it seems to disturb any attempt at a teleological understanding that would see its elements or "motifs" as "compositionally motivated." From what is in fact a formalist position, each would then contribute to bringing about the outcome and would have been chosen in view of it. This implies that the work has at least aesthetic unity in that at its conclusion all its disparate elements are reconciled.[8] This study has attempted to show that, on the contrary, at any one moment several possibilities, perhaps even incompatible ones, coexist within a network of complex and polysemous relationships that does not allow for totalization. Tardieu has even compared the composition of his one act plays to "la démarche créatrice des musiciens lorqu'ils composent à partir d'une volonté abstraite

et non d'une représentation imitative, ni d'une
figuration quelconque."[9] It appears that his technique is to play with a theatrical or linguistic
"object," allowing it to elaborate the multivalent
possibilities of its constitutive elements. Rather
than developing linearly, then, Le Meuble, like an
ornamental grotesque or perhaps a Baroque sonata,
seems to spin out an opening figure from a distinc-
tive thematic pattern, one thing transforming itself
into another while remaining somewhat the same. In
this way it, like the grotesque in general, calls
into question many of the basic concepts on which
the classical perception of reality, is grounded--a
perception which, to a large extent, is still our
own.[10]

NOTES

[1]See, for example, Lee Byron Jennings, The
Ludicrous Demon: Aspects of the Grotesque in German
Post-Romantic Prose (Berkeley: University of
California Publications in Modern Philology, vol.
71, 1963), pp. 19, 22. The notion of the grotesque
on which the present discussion is based is further
elaborated in my article, "La Forme In-Formante: A
Reconsideration of the Grotesque," Mosaic, 14(4),
pp. 107-121.

[2]Vitruvius Pollio, The Ten Books on Architecture,
trans. Morris Hicky Morgan (1914; reprint ed.,
New York: Dover Publications, Inc., 1960), 7(5),
p. 211.

[3]Jean Tardieu, Le Meuble, in his Théâtre de
Chambre (Paris: Gallimard, 1966), p. 40. Future
references will be included in the body of the text.

[4]Sigmund Freud, Jokes and Their Relation to the
Unconscious, trans. J. Strachey (1960; reprint ed.,
New York: W. W. Norton & Co., 1963), pp. 117-158.

[5]Sigmund Freud, "The Uncanny," in On Creativity
and the Unconscious, ed. B. Nelson (New York:
Harper and Row, Harper Colophon Books, 1958),
p. 145.

[6]Sigmund Freud, _Beyond the Pleasure Principle_,
trans. J. Strachey (1959; reprint ed., New York:
W. W. Norton & Co., 1961), p. 32.

[7]Henri Bergson, _Le Rire_ (Paris: Librairie Félix
Alcan, 1916), p. 6.

[8]B. Tomachevski, "Thématique," and B. Eikhenbaum,
"Sur la theorie de la prose," in _Théorie de la
littérature_, trans. and ed. T. Todorov (Paris:
Seuil, 1965), pp. 207-8, 282.

[9]Jean Tardieu, "Avant-Propos," _Théâtre de
Chambre_, pp. 7-8.

[10]For a discussion of the various strategies that
have been or could be employed in an effort to
interpret _Le Meuble_, see my article, "Le Meuble:
Tardieu's Grotesque Con-trap-tion," _Stanford French
Review_, 6(1).

5

DEVIL'S DOORWAY AND THE USE OF

GENRE AS DISGUISE

Paul Petlewski

This study is primarily about Anthony Mann's
first western, though my own emphasis is upon issues
that relate the film to a genre other than its own
ostensible one. Devil's Doorway[1] was released in
1950, towards the end of a five-year-period that had
seen the reemergence in commercial filmmaking of the
"social problem" film, a loosely linked group of
pictures that dealt, centrally, with suppressed
problems within American society, at least as it was
normally reflected in film. The concerns of these
films ranged from alcoholism to disabled veterans to
the condition of mental institutions. But the common factor in a number of them was prejudice--
sometimes religious, as in Gentleman's Agreement,
more often racial, as in Pinky, Home of the Brave,
and Intruder in the Dust.
Hollywood approached the racial issue gingerly,
and, given the normal parameters of audience accep-
tance, it did so with good reason. All of these
films, therefore, have two basic ideological compo-
nents. First (what is in effect the exposé element
of the films), they acknowledge bluntly that certain
kinds of prejudice exist in America. Second, they
close by stating, or at least intimating, that these
problems are ultimately solvable, often through a

kind of collective good will, tolerance, or in-
creased understanding.

These endings, often viewed today as a concession
to soft liberalism or audience wish-fulfillment fan-
tasies, were of course absolutely necessary. The
films were dealing with subject matter of such potential volatility--racial hatred--and had such un-
certain commercial prospects that the risk of vio-
lating audience expectations involving closure was
very real. The endings of these pictures labor to
contain, to defuse, those very problems which the
films themselves have defined as being so deeply in-
grained in America that few other films dare acknowledge their existence--thus the occasional feeling that the endings seem grafted onto the works
rather than being organic.

Theoretically, at any rate, these narratives
could dramatize the problem but refuse to admit the
very possibility of resolution (a film could end,
for instance, by suggesting that blacks and whites
might always exist in a situation of prejudice and
hostility). Or a narrative could resolve the problem by eliminating or suppressing one of the groups;
at its most extreme this is the genocide solution
which, two decades later, would be explicit in such
accusatory "westerns" as Little Big Man and Soldier
Blue.

In 1950, though, probably only one approach was
commercially feasible: unpalatable endings might be
softened when such material could be disguised within the familiar and relatively comfortable confines
of a different genre, the subtext disguised (and
well-disguised) by the text. It is within such a
framework that I would like to consider some elements of Devil's Doorway, which contains a smuggled
assessment of racial relations in America. Now this
is really nothing particularly new; in his monograph
Westerns, Philip French notes that "the Indian has
often been a surrogate Negro in numerous liberal
Westerns of the 1950s."[2] But Devil's Doorway stands
in a significant position as one of the very first
such films; its historical importance has been
effaced by the appearance that same year of a more
famous and popular (and conventional) western,
Broken Arrow, whose central character is white. And
more important--the aspect that is new--Devil's
Doorway provides a resolution of racial tension that

is radically different from those of, say, <u>Pinky</u> or
<u>Home of the Brave</u>, a vision so bleak and pessimistic
that it could not possibly have been permitted within a contemporary setting. (It is surprising enough
to note that the film was produced by MGM, a studio
not noted for providing bleak visions, disguised or
otherwise.) Anthony Mann's films are often painful
to watch because their heroes are so racked by extreme and incompatible impulses. But <u>Devil's Door-</u>
<u>way</u> stands as his only picture which is itself
racked by incompatible impulses: its liberal desire
for a resolution evoking fellowship and harmony on
the one hand versus an apocalyptic vision involving
the annihilation of a race on the other. Mann's
film eventually solves the racial problem in a manner which is very rare for the '50s: it kills off
all the Indians.

Now come the qualifications that should be made
concerning that last sentence. The film does not
of course advocate genocide--the point is that it
dares to envision and then actually to play out that
possibility. In fact, its main character is an
Indian named Broken Lance (though played by a white
actor, Robert Taylor) who returns to Shoshone tribal
land following his service with the Union Army. He
is treated by the film, up to a certain point, with
immense sympathy and respect, as are the other
Indians.

Moreover, not all the Indians are literally
killed in the final battle. Some, mostly women and
children, are allowed to go to a reservation, the
fate which they have been resisting through the
whole movie. But the Shoshones' own land has been
defined as a condition of their existence quite
explicitly--and repeatedly--during the course of the
film. Broken Lance's father tells him that "an
Indian without land loses his soul." Towards the
end of the film Broken Lance himself speaks of the
meaning of the Shoshone land: "If we lose it now we
might as well all be dead." And his last words,
just before falling dead at the feet of an Army
officer are, "We're all gone."

It is a truly pessimistic climax; the only gestures that might be termed "hopeful" in this film
are centered on the future, much like that final
title in Samuel Fuller's <u>Run of the Arrow</u>: "The end
of this story can only be written by you." And

those gestures occur in two lines of dialogue that
are ostensibly addressed to other characters but are
in fact aimed directly at the viewer. In one--a
sequence shot like a love scene but which exists to
assert the impossibility of interracial love, a sequence I'll return to--Broken Lance looks at the
white heroine and says, "A hundred years from now it
might have worked." The other gesture is the last
line of the picture, spoken by the heroine: "It
would be too bad if we ever forgot."
     Now the situation in which Broken Lance finds
himself is central to many of Mann's major films,
all those pictures in which the heroes are torn between two ways of life, two identities. We have the
gunman turned farmer at the end of Bend of the River
and the beginning of Man of the West, the farmer
turned bounty hunter in The Naked Spur, the primitive man of nature turned U.S. soldier in The Last
Frontier, the soldier turned rebel in The Fall of
the Roman Empire, the citizen turned patriot, turned
exile, turned legend in El Cid. But in Devil's
Doorway that tension is never resolved. It is there
at the beginning, when the hero (known by his white
Army name of Lance Poole) rides into town wearing
cowboy clothes--only to be identified as an Indian
when a small dog rushes into the street, barking,
yipping, snapping at his horse's legs. And it is
still there at the end, when Broken Lance, surrounded by soldiers and murderous whites, removes his
Indian garb, dons his old Union uniform, pins on
his Congressional Medal of Honor, walks outside, and
is shot dead.
     The film builds toward this conclusion in what
might be considered a conventional narrative fashion, by systematically eliminating every other possible alternative to either violence or abject sur-
render. Thus all of Broken Lance's legal claims are
summarily rejected, thus the voices of reason and
tolerance in the white community (like the crusty
old sheriff) are silenced by guns, thus the sympa-
thetic soldiers are rendered helpless by "orders"
and "the law." But there is another, more curious
element in the film that renders this ending necessary. I have already mentioned that the picture
celebrates its hero "up to a point." In fact, very
late in the running time, Devil's Doorway begins to

have reservations about Broken Lance's status as
"hero."

Here is an example, the first of two scenes. For
most of the picture Broken Lance has been a model of
patience and restraint, an advocate of that law
which he once fought for. But eventually, under-
standably, he turns savage and bitter: he ambushes
the film's chief villain and strangles him. And it
is at this moment, I think, that any viewer reason-
ably conversant with the conventions of the classical narrative film will realize that Broken Lance is
not going to survive the film. For the chief
villain happens to be an old man, quite unable to
match the Indian physically. What might be summa-
rized on paper as a struggle looks, on film, like a
murder--or, at best, an execution. At this moment,
no matter how understandable or logical his action
may be in the abstract, Broken Lance violates one of
the really crucial generic conventions of the
western: the principle of the fair fight. And, in
doing so, he has suddenly introduced into the film
many of the qualities associated with the "bad"
movie Indian--sneakiness, Indian cunning, ruthless-
ness, a lack of fair play--stereotypes which the
film, in its early stages, has seemed anxious to
erase.

And there is a second element that the film seems
even more nervous about: the possibility of the
Indian as sexual threat. Now one of the obligatory
ingredients of the western, at least during this
period, is a love story. Devil's Doorway sets up
all the conventional situations that signal "love
story" and then backs away, refusing to let them
gel. Hero and heroine even "meet cute"--Broken
Lance goes off to consult the town lawyer about
Indian land claims and is distressed and embarrassed
when he discovers this town lawyer is a woman. The
film then takes a good deal of time and care (there
is virtually no physical action at its center) de-
lineating the growth of mutual esteem and admiration
--though the two avoid real physical contact. This
culminates in a scene previously referred to. The
two are trapped in a cabin surrounded by soldiers,
they turn to each other, move closer. The film
dutifully cuts from medium shots to close ups, an-
ticipating their first kiss. And that kiss never
comes. Instead, doubt, hesitancy, and perhaps fear

appear, especially on the heroine's face, and the
two turn away. Now whether the failure of this
abortive romance is a logical outgrowth of the relationship and the trying circumstances that surround it (which is quite possible) or whether the
film itself has become wary of the sexual/racial
implication of the strong Indian dominating the
white lady is a question which must, I think, remain open. One can say, though, that westerns
generally evince a preference for white men taking
Indian brides (as in Broken Arrow) rather than
Indians taking white brides.

   At any rate, it seems likely from the two scenes
just mentioned that the film is trying to find some
way, not exactly to justify, but to soften the
impact of Broken Lance's death, to render it as
tragic but inevitable. For, finally, what other
choice does the film have? Broken Lance is not
just a helpless Indian victim, set up to be mur-
dered by villainous whites; he is a very highly
skilled soldier. The alternative to killing him
(for he quite obviously is not going to march off
quietly to the reservation) is to allow all of his
skill and courage and savagery to be unleashed
against the white man, perhaps in a kind of guerilla
war. And this the film, despite its acknowledgment,
time and again, of the prejudice visited upon the
Indian, is not quite prepared to allow. We come
back to a central tenet of the classical narrative
film: a film's climax must contain or suppress the
unmanageable forces, the excess energy, which that
film has generated. Better, finally, that Broken
Lance die and let characters say how terrible this
all is and how we should never forget. A sad ending, perhaps--but a very conclusive one.

   Part of the interest of Devil's Doorway stems
from its historical context, from observing how a
genre piece could deal, covertly, with sensitive
subject matter in a way more daring, more extreme
(even given the compromises just mentioned) than
could more famous films. In concluding, though, I
should note that the use of genre as disguise is
today virtually impossible, for the existence of a
"disguised" genre piece is of course contingent upon that work being surrounded by many absolutely
ordinary genre films. The fact is that we may have
reached a point in film history where an essentially

innocent, ordinary genre piece can no longer exist;
that is, a movie which can be made without taking
into account (and taking into account with great
deliberation and self-consciousness) previous works
of the genre as well as the political and sexual and
economic climate in which that film is made. When,
rarely, such a film does emerge, like Fuller's The
Big Red One, it has the feel of something recovered
from a time capsule.

   Today--still taking the western as a general
example, partially because there are so few of them
made--we have occasional films which are meditations
upon their own status as westerns: Monte Hellman's
films and Robert Altman's two efforts in the genre,
McCabe and Mrs. Miller and Buffalo Bill and the
Indians. Much more frequently we have films which
seem to exist primarily as reactions to or comments
upon previous works in the genre: secondary sources
responding, often at great distance, to the primary
texts. Two of 1980s three period westerns stand in
precisely this position: The Long Riders churning
up The Wild Bunch and previous Jesse James movies,
Tom Horn looking like a bizarre Thomas McGuane re-
working of The Missouri Breaks on the one hand and,
on the other, a return to those revisionist, deter-
ministic westerns of the early seventies, where to
be a cowboy is to die.

   Even if some essentially innocent genre filmmakers still remain, then there are certainly no
longer such creatures as innocent film readers. And
the combination of all these factors tends to elimi-
nate the possibility of disguise. Those two "westerns" that I alluded to earlier--Little Big Man and
Soldier Blue--cannot really be treated as disguised
versions of socio-political commentary; both of them
were read immediately as being "about" Vietnam. We
have now a situation in which what might once have
been considered a subtext (as in Devil's Doorway,
not a very self-conscious movie) explodes through
the surface and becomes the text. This may not be
a bad thing for art, but it probably does not bode
well for the strictly commercial future of such
genres as the western.

NOTES

[1]Devil's Doorway begins as its Indian hero,
Broken Lance, returns to his tribal land following
very distinguished service during the Civil War.
He encounters prejudice in the white community and
a long (ultimately successful) attempt to open
Indian land to white settlers and send the Indians
to a reservation. When Broken Lance and his fellow
Indians finally take up arms, they are all shot
dead.

[2]Philip French, Westerns (New York: The Viking
Press, 1973), p. 95.

6

THE STRUCTURE OF TRANSFORMATION IN

MICHEL BUTOR'S LA MODIFICATION

Patricia Struebig

Any interpretation of La Modification requires
the use of a critical method which can take into
account the narrative complexity of the text. This
problem is resolved by the choice of Claude Lévi-
Strauss's method for the structural analysis of
myth. The method facilitates the analysis of the
apparent temporal confusion of La Modification by
allowing the researcher to reveal the synchronic
and diachronic dimensions of the tale. In this
work, Butor's novel is treated as a contemporary
myth, according to the definition given to the term
by Lévi-Strauss: Léon Delmont attempts to recognize
and to admit to an "insurmountable contradiction."
Such an admission and the consequent resolution of
the conflict are, according to the ethnologist, the
functions of myth.
    A brief review of the action of the novel exposes
the elements of the mythic tale which are needed to
reveal its structure. Léon Delmont's wish to leave
his wife for his mistress is banal in appearance,
but in fact hides a deeper conflict. The mythic,
universal dimension of the conflict exists in the
multiple versions of the story which are proposed
by the hero's mind during his nocturnal train trip
from Paris to Rome.

The apparent content of the novel, in its syn-
tagmatic form (that is, the description of the nocturnal trip) is reorganized in paradigms. For
example:

> Paris   v. Rome
> Henriette v. Cécile
> Vieille vie v. Nouvelle vie
> (Old life)   (New life)

The analysis of these oppositions reveals the mediation attempts by means of which the latent meaning
of the story is brought to light.

Léon Delmont is not merely seeking a new life
with a new woman. His true goal is himself, the
"new" Léon. He is seeking renewal through an internal and personal quest. He wishes to find himself
again in his age of "authenticité," but he can only
achieve this by overcoming all the obstacles and by
passing through all the stages of a mythic quest in
the underworld. The "vérité négative" (negative
truth) which is an insurmountable contradiction for
him, is to accept the failure of his life, and to
admit that he himself has been the cause.

The schema of the "global integration" of our
proposed structure for the novel illustrates the
reciprocal relationship between mobility, immobility, and the quest:

INTEGRATION DES SCHEMES:

QUETE

MOBILITE   IMMOBILITE

The mediating term of the "quest" is located between
the extremes of movement and immobility, and ini-
tiates the progressive action toward the resolution
of the contradiction, toward "la prise de con-
science." Thus, the three states coexist, and their
reciprocal action leads the hero toward his goal,
self awareness, for being mobile while remaining

immobile causes the interior quest. Testing this
conclusion by applying the mathematical formula created by Lévi-Strauss for this purpose allows us to
express the "vérité négative" that the mythic hero
of <u>La</u> <u>Modification</u> has hidden from himself: the renewal he seeks does not lie outside himself. He
will rediscover his "être ancien et durable" by
ridding himself of his falseness, his "être
inauthentique." The final proposition of the formula expresses what once was inexpressible: Léon
must "move while remaining immobile" . . . external
immobility (maintaining the same life in appearance)
covers internal mobility (continuing always to
change himself, to seek, to move toward a new and
sincere life, "une vie d'authenticité").

The mythic quality of the tale is thus proven,
for the apparently simple role of one man is transformed into a universal symbol.

Before attempting the application of Lévi-
Strauss's formula to the schema of our novel's
structure, we first must recapitulate its action.
The formula,

$$f_x(a) \quad : \quad f_y(b) \quad : \quad : \quad f_x(b) \quad : \quad f_{a-1}(y)^1$$

according to Lévi-Strauss, expresses the "loi du
mythe," thus rendering the latent meaning of the
mythic tale comprehensible to the reader. He reads
the homology as: "the relationship between $f_x(a)$ and
$f_y(b)$ compares with the relationship between $f_x(b)$
and $f_{a-1}(y)$." To understand this process one must
refer to some basic elements of the structural study
of myth according to Lévi-Strauss:

1. "Mythic thought proceeds from the recognition of
    certain oppositions and tends toward their pro-
    gressive mediation." This process, as occurring
    in <u>La</u> <u>Modification</u>, is represented as follows:

INTEGRATION DES NIVEAUX:
LA STRUCTURE DE LA MEDIATION

Paire initiale	Première triade	Deuxième triade
QUITTER		
	DEPLACER	
	TRANSPOSER	
		RETOURNER
		RETROUVER
		RENAITRE
	REUNIR	
TROUVER		

2. Lévi-Strauss's formula describes the "law of
    myth." That is, it describes the schema of the
    global integration.
3. In rendering on a manifest level the operating
    function of the myth, the formula discloses to
    the reader the sense of the "non-sense" of the
    mythic tale. That is, comparing the relation-
    ships between the two pairs of elements in the
    formula teaches us the meaning of a tale with a
    mythological structure: the relationship between
    $f_x(a)$ and $f_y(b)$ compares with the relationship
    between $f_x(b)$ and $f_{a-1}(y)$. Thus the formula
    helps the reader to deconstruct the process which
    created the tale that he is attempting to under-
    stand. The text of the tale exists as such, but
    what it communicates to the reader is not clear;

there is a fault, a lack, a non-sense in the communication. Understanding the mechanism which
has formed the tale, including the fault, means
understanding the sense of non-sense, the sense
of what is missing in the enunciation. Daniel
Patte, in "Structural Network in Narrative,"
explains the action thus:

> When the mechanism of the phenomenon of com-
> munication begins to be known by the analyst,
> he can then use this knowledge in an attempt
> at remedying defective communication of mean-
> ing, e.g., when a text is not fully meaning-
> ful for the reader.[2]

Each element of the formula represents the relation of an action with a state. By inserting the
content of the integrated tables, Intégration des
Niveaux, (p. 50) plus Intégration des Schèmes (p. 48)
into the formula, we discover the following relationships:

$$f_x(a) \quad : \quad f_y(b) \quad : : \quad f_x(b) \quad : \quad f_{a-1}(y)$$

quitter$^{(Paris)}$, trouver$^{(Rome)}$ quitter$^{(Rome)}$ (se)   (avoir
                                                          déplacer trouvé,
                                                          [non-Pariser] être
                                                                    arrivé)

établir le conflit   tentative   état   3
                              de médiation   final
                              du conflit

In "Structural Models in Folklore," Elli Köngäs
Maranda and Paul Maranda point out this "non-linear"
quality of Lévi-Strauss's formula. There are three
stages in their explanation of the formula's mechan-
ics: establishment of the conflict, attempt at mediation, and final state. Concerning this last stage
they tell us that:

> The final result is not merely a cyclical re-
> turn to the point of departure after the first
> force has been nullified but a helicoidal
> step, a new situation different from the ini-
> tial one not only in that it nullifies it but

also because it consists of a state which is
more than a nullification of the initial.[4]

In order to find the meaning of a^{-1}, we refer
again to Patte's interpretation. What Lévi-Strauss
calls "the inverse of a" (a^{-1}), Patte designates
"non-a" ($\bar{a}$). He identifies "non-a" by its relationship of contradictory of "a" in the semiotic square,
which he introduces as follows:

> The structure often called the semiotic square
> is nothing other than Aristotle's logical
> square. Any semantic feature has both a con-
> trary and a contradictory: life has the con-
> trary death and the contradictory non-life
> (e.g., non-living matter). There is also a
> relation of implication between the contrary
> and the contradictory: thus death implies
> non-life. If we consider the opposition in
> terms of the other pole of the opposition of
> contraries--death--we find that it has also
> a contradictory--death has as its contradic-
> tory non-death--and we find another relation
> of implication--life implies non-death. Thus
> we have the square:

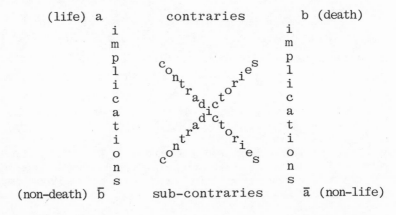

According to Pate, a and b (or x and y of our formula) are contraries, while a and $\bar{a}$ (a^{-1} of our formula) are contradictories. That is, life is the contrary of death, but the "contradictory" (the inverse) of life would be non-life (non-living matter).

In analyzing the details of Léon's multiple
trips, we have chosen three versions as representa-
tive of the attempts to mediate the contradiction in
his life. These versions are schematized in the
following figure, "Les Niveaux," the levels of the
mythological tale:

Les Niveaux

I. Le Voyage   II. Le Voyage imaginé

Paris	Rome	Rome	Rome
Henriette	Cécile		Paris
Vieille vie	Nouvelle vie	Cécile	Cécile + Léon
Travail	Loisir	Vieux Léon	Léon rajeuni
Fatigue	Repos	Loisir volé	Travail + loisir
Nuit	Jour		

III. Le Voyage projeté

Rome	Rome dans Paris (retrouver Paris)
Cécile	Cécile dans Henriette (retrouver Henriette)
Nouvelle vie	Nouvelle vie dans ancienne vie (renaître)
Vieux Léon	Nouveau Léon en lui-même (se retrouver)

Our interpretation of Lévi-Strauss's formula, illustrated by inserting as its functions and terms the
hypotheses of our analysis of the text, is explained
as follows:

(a)   = (Paris), symbol of the static state.
(a^{-1}) = (non-Paris), symbol of the mobile or
         changing state (the inverse of the static
         state).
a^{-1}, as a function, is then to "de-Paris" or
         become "de-Parised," the action of dis-
         placing (oneself), of changing.

The same procedure reveals the significance of (y),
that is y, the function, permuted to (y), the term.

y   = to find, in the sense of to seek some-
         thing (action, role).

(y),   as a state of being or symbol, is the
result of the action y.[6]

The result of the role "to find" is to have found
something, to have arrived at the end of the quest.
The reading of the fourth element of the formula is
then: by displacing oneself (to displace oneself =
to no longer be static, old, bourgeois, "Parisian"),
one arrives (one finds oneself).

The relationship between the function and the
term in each element of the formula is that of de-
fining an action based on a problem which is inherent
in the tale. A reading of the propositions, inserting the vocabulary of the tale, would be:

$f_x(a)$ (to be "in Paris" poses a problem for you),
therefore you must leave this city.

$f_y(b)$ (not being "in Rome" poses a problem for
you), therefore you must go there [go to
find "Rome"].

$f_x(b)$:   mediation; an attempt at bringing these
opposed situations closer together.

$f_x(b)$ (you would like to be "in Rome"), whereas
you leave this city.

$f_{a-1}(y)$ (you [would like] wish to have found some-
thing--yourself--to have arrived at the end
of your quest), therefore you must not remain "Parisian." You must become de-
Parised: you must no longer be "old,"
static, attached to your possessions and
money--bourgeois. In order to find oneself,
to arrive, one must displace oneself, be
"mobile," seek: one must be mobile in immobility (change within, while maintaining
the same appearance without).

It is in this last element of the formula that the
apparent and the latent, the literal and the figura-
tive, unite.

What is told by our mythological tale is symbolically expressed by the role played by Paris (symbol
of the static, old, "dead" state of Léon's life),
that is, the force exerted by "Paris" (when this
symbol is transformed into a role) on the symbolized
action of "finding." One must become "de-Parised"
in order "to be found," "to have arrived." Léon
Delmont tells us that all his peregrinations, all
his travails, all his reflection lead him to a goal:

to the act of writing a book (symbol of the life of a
man) in which he will show the role that Rome (symbol
of youth, liberty, new life) can play in the life of
a man in Paris (symbol of old age, ties, death).
Analyzing his words according to our interpretation
of Lévi-Strauss's formula reveals that (see figures,
pp. 51 and 53):

1. (Rome and Paris) are terms in the first proposi-
    tion of the formula. What is symbolized by Rome,
    then, is opposed to what is symbolized by Paris.
    By referring to the table of the levels (Les
    Niveaux, p. 53), the meaning of these two symbols
    and of their opposition is recognized.
2. The mathematic functioning of the formula renders
    the latent meaning of Léon's words explicit.
    Again in the table of Niveaux, we find that there
    are efforts to fuse the image of Rome with the
    image of Paris. This mediation attempt is ex-
    pressed by $f_{x(b)}$. Rome is now "to be left," but
    in the sense of attempting to bring it to Paris,
    in a way to superimpose this city upon Paris.
3. The resolution of the conflict is expressed by
    the fourth element of the formula, result of the
    dynamic action of the mediation process.

Exchanging Paris for Rome is not possible. Physically displacing the elements of one city to unite
it with the other is no more possible. The only possible solution, then, presents itself: that of changing completely while remaining the same. External
immobility (keeping the same life in appearance)
covers internal mobility (being continually in the
process of changing, of seeking oneself, of advancing
toward a new life of sincerity, of "authenticité."
It is true then that the formula describes the
"law of myth," for it brings to a manifest level what
is expressed by the mythological structure of La
Modification: moving from one city to another, from
one woman to another, from one life to another is
not essential, but rather it is that this act becomes symbolic. By comparing the two propositions
of the formula, one can recognize the meaning of the
relationship between these two pairs of opposed relations. Leaving Paris in order to find Rome (completely rejecting one way of life in order to begin
another) expresses, in fact, what appears to be a

non-sense: leaving Rome (supposedly the ideal, the achievement of happiness) in order "to find oneself" through this act.

Analyzing this non-sense, this lack of the system of communication, rejuvenates the very old theme of "leaving one's wife for one's mistress." Leaving Rome, an act which seems the contrary of what the hero seeks, means in fact, attempting to bring the two cities, the two ways of life, closer together. And this act, lived by the hero in his strolls through the labyrinth of Paris, of Rome, and in the train trip between the two cities, symbolizes the last relationship: displacing oneself (being mobile) in immobility (having arrived)--that is, shedding one's insincere self while still maintaining the appearances of this self, or, in the words of Léon Delmont, rediscovering "one's former and lasting being," being reborn.

NOTES

[1]Claude Lévi-Strauss, Anthropologie Structurale (Paris: Plon, 1958), pp. 252-253.

[2]Daniel Patte, "Structural Network in Narrative: The Good Samaritan," Soundings 58 (1975): 222.

[3]Elli Köngäs Maranda and Paul Maranda, Structural Models in Folklore and Transformational Essays (The Hague and Paris: Mouton, 1971), pp. 25-28.

[4]Ibid., p. 26.

[5]Patte, "Structural Network," pp. 235-236.

[6]Ibid., p. 237.

7

A FAILURE OF TRANSFORMATION: THE FEMININE

ARCHETYPE IN BERGMAN'S

CRIES AND WHISPERS

Barbara F. McManus

Not all films stand in a direct, unequivocal relation to social reality; the films of Ingmar
Bergman, in fact, are particularly problematic in
this regard. Although Scenes from a Marriage re-
sponds readily to a realistic approach and The
Seventh Seal seems to demand a symbolic interpretation, the role of reality in many of Bergman's other
films is not so easily discernible. Cries and
Whispers, for example, combines a starkly realistic
depiction of the physical agonies of a dying woman
with a dreamlike scene in which the dead woman weeps,
speaks, and even touches the other characters. Which
scene sets the tone for the film? Is the film primarily realistic or symbolic? Critics' answers to
this question have profoundly affected their interpretations of the film.
    The assumption that Cries and Whispers attempts
to reflect social reality directly has led feminist
critics to reject the film. Molly Haskell decries
its "furtive misogyny,"[1] while Joan Mellen is sharply
critical of its portrayal of women: "Far from understanding and showing compassion for the plight of
women, Bergman creates female characters who are
given the choice--only as in Cries and Whispers--to

be a Karin, cold and frigid, or a Maria (mindless and
promiscuous) or an Agnes, inexplicably non-
heterosexual and insatiably in angst or an Anna, ser-
vile and bovine. And Bergman implies through the
closed microcosm of human existence he presents that
these will forever be our alternatives. . . . Cries
and Whispers, in fact, provides one of the most
retrograde portrayals of women on the contemporary
screen."2 This realistic approach, however, fails
to account for the powerful effect of the film, at-
tested to by Vincent Canby in the closing words of
his review of the film in the New York Times (22
Dec. 1972, p. 16, col. 1): "Cries and Whispers . . .
is not an easy film to describe or to endure. It
stands alone and it reduces everything else you're
likely to see this season to the size of a small
cinder." Pauline Kael attributes this effect to the
symbolic rather than realistic nature of the film,
comparing it to the dream plays of August Strindberg
and the hauntingly evocative paintings of Edvard
Munch: "Cries and Whispers has oracular power, and
many people feel that when something grips them
strongly it must be realistic; they may not want to
recognize that being led into a dreamworld can move
them so much. But I think it's the stylized-dream-
play atmosphere of Cries and Whispers that has made
it possible for Bergman to achieve such strength."3
    Although there are realistic elements in the
film, I tend to agree with Kael that Cries and
Whispers must be interpreted symbolically in order
to perceive its full depth and power. It is difficult to imagine a film more drastically cut off from
society than this one is. The time and place are
never precisely specified, although the atmosphere
is vaguely turn of the century. All the action takes
place inside a large manor house or (in brief flash-
backs) in its surrounding park. The color scheme is
intrusive and extremely stylized, dominated by red,
white, and black, with all the interiors decorated
in shades of red and all scene transitions accom-
plished by red fade-outs. The pace is slow and
trancelike, with long pauses and close-ups, while
much of the action is improbable at best. But the
most telling aspect of the film in this respect is
its complete lack of any sense of the complex network
of social relations that helps to define an individual. The characters appear to have no past, no life

outside the manor house. Although we are told that
Karin's husband is a diplomat, this fact is totally
irrelevant to the film. The actions of these characters are not "motivated" in any ordinary sense of the
term; we do not see them as affected by or as affect-
ing their social environment. Even the nature of
Agnes's illness is never specified. We are simply
asked to accept the characters as they are and to
perceive their interrelationships.

Thus, it appears, Bergman has deliberately sev-
ered us from our sense of reality in order to stress
the symbolic validity rather than the verisimilitude
of his characters. But once we have acknowledged the
symbolic nature of the film, how should we interpret
it? It is not enough to say with Pauline Kael that
"the four women of Cries and Whispers are used as
obsessive male visions of women . . . as the Other,
women as the mysterious, sensual goddess of male
fantasy," for "to keep scanning woman as the Other
doesn't get any of us anywhere."[4] I believe that
Cries and Whispers is not so much a symbolic portrayal of "woman" as it is an exploration of the
nature of feminine symbolism. Thus the central
characters in the film are archetypes rather than
stereotypes, and they relate to symbolic tendencies
prevalent in dreams, myth, art, and literature rather
than to actual women.

This feminine archetypal symbolism imposes its
own structure on Cries and Whispers, providing an
inner cohesiveness and significance below the level
of the film's rather simplistic story line. There
are remarkable correspondences between the archetypal symbolism as it appears in this film and the
structure of the feminine archetype as analyzed by
Erich Neumann, a friend and student of Carl Jung, in
his perceptive study The Great Mother: An Analysis of
the Archetype.[5] According to Neumann, there are four
polar female figures within the feminine archetype:
the positive and negative elementary figures (the
Good Mother and the Old Witch or Terrible Mother) and
the positive and negative transformative figures (the
Virgin and the Young Witch or Seductress). Each of
these figures has its own characteristic appearance,
function, and cluster of symbols, and each can be
transformed into its opposite. I believe that the
four women in Cries and Whispers draw their symbolic
life from these four figures; their interaction in

the film explores the potential for transformation
within the feminine archetype. I do not mean to
suggest that Bergman was actually influenced by
Neumann's work or deliberately set out to dramatize
the feminine archetype; it is, after all, part of
the very nature of archetypal symbolism that it
usually operates below the threshold of conscious
awareness. In fact, in the story of Cries and
Whispers that he published in the New Yorker (21
Oct. 1972), Bergman himself stated that the film
arose out of an image that haunted him for more than
a year, a mind-picture of four women in flowing white
dresses.[6] This, as well as his inability to explain
the obsessive color scheme of the film ("Don't ask
me why it must be so, because I don't know"[7]), suggests that Bergman drew upon strong unconscious symbolic impulses in creating this film.

These symbolic impulses link Cries and Whispers
with a large body of archetypal myth, literature,
and art. However, these usually present the feminine archetype in relation to the male (as hero, son,
lover, or male companion), while Cries and Whispers
dramatizes the inner dynamics of the archetype, the
feminine turned in upon itself rather than transforming or destroying the male. The four male characters in the film are truly peripheral figures,
present solely to help define the symbolic roles of
the females. Their actions do not affect the women,
nor are they at all changed by the women (even
Maria's husband, shown in flashback stabbing himself
because of her infidelity, appears at the end of the
film completely unscathed and unchanged). Although
a mother and an aunt appear briefly in flashback,
there is no suggestion of a father in the film, and
even the children are all female. The film's setting
and atmosphere are almost oppressively feminine, as
the drama unfolds in the red, womblike interiors of
a house surrounded by nature rather than society,
with all actions taking place around tables or beds.
(According to Neumann, the house, table, and bed are
the "central symbols which constellate female domina-
tion inside the family."[8])

Each of the four women in the film represents a
different aspect of the feminine archetype, as revealed through color and appearance, imagery, and
action. The film is structured very symmetrically,
being composed of a series of discrete scenes dif-

ferentiated by red fade-outs; each of these scenes,
in turn, is built around one of the women and serves
to define her archetypal role. Each woman dominates
one flashback and one scene in the present (excluding
Anna, who has no flashback), and all these scenes
then culminate in the surrealistic sequence (presented as Anna's dream) where the corpse speaks to the
women one by one. All the women, dressed in white,
share the opening scene and the flashback which
closes the film. This structure emerges very clearly
when the eleven scenes are presented schematically:

                    9–Anna, dream sequence

                  8–Karin, present

                7–Maria, present

              6–Karin, flashback

          5–Agnes, present   10–Epilogue, present

        4–Anna, present

      3–Maria, flashback

    2–Agnes, flashback

1–Opening scene,   11–Final scene,
   present   Four Women in White   flashback

The very symmetry of this film's structure leads the
viewer to analyze the differing roles of the women
and highlights the correspondences with the four polar figures in Neumann's discussion of the feminine
archetype.
     The film focuses first on Agnes, who is clearly
associated with the positive transformative figure
of the feminine archetype, the Virgin. Although the
transformative symbolism of the feminine is grounded
in the archetypal tendency to personify sexuality as
feminine, the most positive of the transformative
figures are virginal ones, females who represent the
sublimation of sexual urges to less physical ends.
Here are the least earthly feminine symbols, surrounded by images of whiteness, purity, and innocence, associated with inspiration, religion, wisdom, and art (Athene, Mary, the Muses). In Cries
and Whispers it is these images which link Agnes
with the figure of the Virgin. Pale and submissive,
Agnes is the least sensual of the four women; she is

the only actual virgin among the four and the only one who is dressed consistently in white throughout the film. She is vaguely artistic; at one point we are shown her rather ethereal painting of a white flower. Her flashback (scene 2), instead of focusing on her face as the others do, begins with a close-up of a white rose; this scene reveals not only her wisdom and delicacy as a child but also the essential loneliness of her character. This loneliness of Agnes is a part of her symbolic role, for the positive transformative figure, as Virgin, is by definition isolated from males and is cut off from the other, more earthy aspects of the feminine by her spiritual nature. In this flashback, then, Agnes remembers a brief contact with her mother, the only moment of closeness she was ever able to achieve with a woman whose sensuality drew her closer to Maria than to Agnes. Later in the film Agnes dominates a scene in the present (scene 5), her death scene, which demonstrates the sweetness of her temperament in suffering. At the end of this scene, after her death, her religious nature is revealed by the priest, who contrasts the depth of her faith with his own sterile doubts.

But Agnes is not presented in a wholly positive light. Although her illness is never explained in the film, Bergman in his story tells us that she is dying of cancer of the uterus, a kind of ironic sublimation of female sexual function. Indeed, she is physically repellent in her death throes, so that her spirituality appears to be bought at the cost of bodily disease and decay. Nevertheless, it is Agnes, with her anguished loneliness and ceaseless reaching for human contact, who serves as the catalyst which brings together the four feminine figures; it is she who provides the only possibility for transformation within the archetypal symbolism of the film.

The youngest sister, Maria, is the polar opposite of Agnes, representing the Seductress or negative transformative figure. At this symbolic pole "we find the alluring and seductive figures of fatal enchantment,"[9] the _femmes fatales_ who use their sexual fascination to diminish, enslave, and destroy (Aphrodite, Astarte, Circe, the Lorelei). These figures are characterized by imagery of negative sexual ecstasy, intoxication, madness, and impotence; they are particularly associated with red as the color of

passion. The beautiful and childish Maria, with her
flaming red hair and lush body, is presented in Cries
and Whispers as the very embodiment of sexuality.
The cut of her dresses is clearly designed to entice,
and she is constantly touching the other characters,
apparently unable to relate to anyone except through
physical contact. Her flashback (scene 3) occurs
shortly after that of Agnes, emphasizing the contrast
between the symbolic roles of the two women. She can
barely wait for the doctor to finish examining her
dying sister before passionately drawing him to herself, and the camera focuses erotically on her pant-
ing face as a lead-in to her flashback. In this
scene, Maria seduces the doctor when he is called to
the house to attend Anna's fatally ill daughter;
although it is obvious that they have slept together
before, all the sexual initiative in the scene comes
from her. She is shown in an extremely seductive red
dress offering him food and wine; the red wine seems
an image of her intoxicating sexuality. This scene
also reveals her essential coldness, selfishness, and
indifference, as well as the destructiveness of her
sexuality, for her infidelity leads her husband to
stab himself in the chest. When he calls to her for
help, she can only shrink back with revulsion.

Her scene in the present (scene 7) is a counterpart of this flashback, as she seduces Karin, strok-
ing and kissing her, trying to draw her out of her
protective shell of untouchability. This seduction
bears fruit in the following scene, leading to a moment of sensual closeness between the two sisters, a
kind of ballet of touching and caressing. However,
like her first seduction in the film, this also
proves to have negative and destructive consequences,
for the epilogue shows her coldly rejecting the now
vulnerable Karin: "You touched me; don't you remember
that?" "I don't recall every stupid thing!"

The servant, Anna, clearly represents the Good
Mother figure. The positive elementary symbolism of
the feminine is primarily static, associated with the
ideas of containment, protection, and shelter; this
figure "tends to hold fast to everything that springs
from it and to surround it like an eternal substance."10 The Good Mother is characterized by
images of earthiness, natural fertility, and abun-
dant vegetation, flowers, and fruit (Demeter, Isis).
In Cries and Whispers Anna is the only truly maternal

figure; she is constantly feeding and dressing the other characters, and her heavy, matronly body and impassive face recall statues of primitive earth goddesses. Her simplicity is revealed by the child-like prayer she recites near the beginning of the film; significantly, she is shown kneeling before a bowl of fruit, a vase of daisies, and a portrait of her dead daughter. Although she has no flashback in the film, Bergman's story, which was apparently the working script for the movie, envisaged a scene in which she snuggled with her small daughter and Agnes in an improvised, womblike shelter within the house while a thunderstorm raged outside. Anna does, however, dominate a scene in the present (scene 4) which clearly reveals her symbolic function. When the restless Agnes calls her in the night, she assures her, "You don't have to worry when Anna's here"; baring her full breasts, she surrounds Agnes protectively and cuddles her to sleep like a small child.

Like Agnes, however, Anna is not presented in totally positive terms. Her simplicity, slowness, and expressionless face make her appear unthinking, almost mindless; although her devotion to her mis-tress is unwavering, the physical closeness which is all she can offer is not enough to obliterate the loneliness of Agnes.

Finally, the oldest sister, Karin, is the polar opposite of Anna, representing the Terrible Mother. The negative elementary figure reverses the symbol-ism of the positive one. Containment and protection become rejection and captivity; giving birth becomes swallowing back, or devouring and castration; rebirth turns to death as the womb becomes a tomb and the goddess becomes an insatiable, blood-drinking monster (Medusa, Kali, Hecate). Terrible Mother figures are particularly associated with black, as the color of death. Of the four women in Cries and Whispers, Karin has the most forbidding appearance, with her black hair, her cold, arrogant face, and her dark, high-necked dresses. Her flashback (scene 6), occur-ring immediately after the death and laying out of Agnes, begins with a close-up of Karin opening her mouth as if about to scream. Significantly dressed in black, she is shown at dinner with her husband; unlike the erotic meal of Maria and the doctor, how-ever, this dinner resembles a duet of cold hatred,

climaxed by Karin's breaking of her wine glass. The
image of the red wine spreading on the white table-
cloth, surrounded by jagged shards of glass, pre-
figures the shocking scene which follows. After vio-
lently slapping Anna, Karin is almost ritually un-
dressed by the servant, shedding layers of clothing
which appear to encase her body like armor. Then,
saying "It's but a tissue of lies," Karin inserts a
needle-sharp piece of glass into her vagina; when
her husband prepares to get into bed with her, she
spreads her legs, revealing her bloody genitals.
Leering at him, she smears blood on her face and
licks it with her lips. Critics who view Cries and
Whispers as a realistic film have found this scene
to be grossly exaggerated, but interpreted symbolically, it is wholly appropriate to the context of
the film and the symbolic role of Karin. For the
mythic motif of the vagina dentata is a primary symbol of the castrating Terrible Mother goddess; in
the words of Erich Neumann, "the destructive side of
the Feminine, the destructive and deathly womb, appears most frequently in the archetypal form of a
mouth bristling with teeth."[11] Here Karin is literally enacting this mythic motif, becoming a monstrous
parody of the castrating, blood-drinking goddess.

After she has rejected Maria's seductive overtures by shrieking, "I can't stand anyone touching
me," Karin dominates a scene in the present (scene
8), where the dinner with Maria serves as an ironic
counterpart of the earlier dinner with her husband.
Here she engages in a frightening monologue which
reveals her consuming hatred--of herself, of Maria,
of life itself--culminating in a series of screams.
The close-up of her open mouth, with its dark red
lips and white teeth, recalls the vagina dentata motif of her flashback: "The mouth as rending, devouring symbol of aggression is characteristic of the
dangerous negative elementary character of the Feminine."[12] Then, without warning, Karin suddenly ca-
pitulates to Maria's overtures.

It is at this point, when both Maria and Karin
appear to have found a new closeness, that Bergman
stages the climactic scene in the film (scene 9).
Presented as a kind of dream of Anna, the scene opens
with a close-up of Anna's face as she hears the sound
of a child crying. Once again dressed in white (although the two sisters are still in black), Anna dis-

covers that the corpse is weeping. Agnes, representing the positive transformative aspect of the feminine, now seeks to transform the symbolic roles of
the women, calling for a readjustment of relations
within the archetypal feminine. According to
Neumann's analysis of the four polar figures in the
archetype, transformation is possible: "The pole is
not only an end point but also a 'turning point.'"[13]
Indeed, myth and literature often dramatize such
changes; in the Odyssey, for example, Circe begins
as the Seductress who turns Odysseus's men into
beasts and ends as the positive Anima figure who
serves as lover and guide for Odysseus. However,
when Agnes, echoing her death cry ("Can't anyone help
me?"), calls each of the women in turn, instead of
being transformed the women are crystallized in their
former symbolic roles. Karin, given an opportunity
for a positive maternal action, instead coldly rejects Agnes, callously telling her that she does not
love her. Maria, who has so freely bestowed destructive kisses, is asked by Agnes for a positive sensual
contact, but she tears herself from Agnes's embrace
and flees screaming from the room. Only Anna is un-
afraid, once again cradling Agnes against her bared
breast and thigh, and Bergman closes the scene with
a tableau of the two women in white, looking like a
somewhat bizarre Pietà.[14] But even Agnes and Anna
fail to find a transformation. Although the earth
goddesses with whom Anna is associated bring the
promise of rebirth, she can still offer no more than
"a massive mound of comforting flesh."[15] And Agnes
is still locked in her essential isolation; even in
death she is desperately seeking some human contact.
In the words of Bergman, "death is the extreme of
loneliness."[16]
    After this climactic scene, the epilogue (scene
10) merely reiterates the roles of the three remaining women. The final scene brings the film full circle; as in the opening scene, the four women once
again appear together in white, although this time in
flashback. Surrounded by nature in the full richness
of autumn, rocking gently back and forth together on
a swing, the women appear to be the picture of innocence, love, and harmony. The words of Agnes's diary
reinforce this impression as she glories in their
closeness: "Now, for a few minutes, I can experience
perfection." But this scene appears cruelly ironic

after the explosive scenes which have preceded it.
The film has dramatized only a failure of transformation; as the image on the screen dissolves to red,
the four women remain locked in mutually exclusive
archetypal roles, revolving around an eternally static core of feminine symbolism.

NOTES

[1] From Reverence to Rape: The Treatment of Women
in the Movies (New York: Holt, Rinehart, and Winston,
1974), p. 38.

[2] "Cries and Whispers: Bergman and Women," Film
Quarterly (Fall 1973), reprint ed. in Ingmar Bergman:
Essays in Criticism, ed. Stuart M. Kaminsky and
Joseph F. Hill (London: Oxford University Press,
1975), pp. 299, 312.

[3] "Flesh," The New Yorker (6 Jan. 1973), reprint
ed. in Reeling (Boston: Little, Brown and Company,
1976), p. 90.

[4] Kael, pp. 91, 94.

[5] The Great Mother, trans. Ralph Manheim, 2nd ed.,
Bollingen Series 47 (Princeton: Princeton University
Press, 1963). See especially Neumann's diagram of
the feminine archetype (Schema III, facing p. 82)
and Chapters 3, 6, and 7.

[6] Four Stories by Ingmar Bergman, trans. Alan
Blair (New York: Doubleday, 1976), p. 63.

[7] Bergman, p. 60.

[8] Neumann, p. 285.

[9] Neumann, p. 80.

[10] Neumann, p. 25.

[11] Neumann, p. 168.

[12] Neumann, pp. 122-23.

[13] Neumann, p. 76.

[14]Kael, p. 92.
[15]Kael, p. 92.
[16]Bergman, p. 86.

NOVEL INTO FILM: SOME PRELIMINARY

RECONSIDERATIONS

Donald F. Larsson

The remarks set out here are tentative, probing,
a preliminary attempt to categorize and form a structure by which the question of filmed adaptations of
novels can begin to be examined. As a beginning,
these remarks first have to address the dominant
practices of adaptation; therefore, most, though not
all, of my references are to Hollywood films of the
silent era and classic sound period. My concern here
is not with the intrinsic natures of the novel and
the film nor with the perceptual differences in the
relationships of reader to book and spectator to
movie. These questions have been the center of much
--too much--writing on film and literature to date.
Though important, such questions seem to take for
granted why adaptations are made in the first place,
leaving only the how to be described, and in spite
of their focus on the reader and spectator, such
questions usually neglect the extent to which these
people are incorporated into the process of adaptation themselves. We need more than the "politique
des adaptations" called for by Charles Eidsvik,[1] we
need a theory of adaptations based on an accurate
history of the motivations and techniques of adaptations and an examination of how narrative forms are
recoded in order to be transferred to a new medium.
This paper is a first, small step toward that project.

From at least the 1920s on--the time when "Hollywood" had secured its hegemony over cinematic prac-
tice--the novel has not only had to share or cede its
position as the dominant American middle class narrative form, it has also had its texts appropriated and
transformed--adopted and adapted--by its rival. Com-
parison of films and novels, especially in the examination of the process of adaptation, has long been
a subject for family talks, after-movie barroom con-
versations, reviewers' tirades, authors' laments,
and learned conferences and publications. Yet too
often these comparisons, whether on the personal, the
popular, or the professional level, have returned to
the same old (not necessarily compatible) clichés:
that Hollywood automatically degrades anything it
touches by reducing it to the lowest common denomi-
nator; that great novels make only mediocre films;[2]
that film and literature are so different that they
cannot be justly compared at all.[3] More recently, a
new set of clichés has come into being, based on the
fact that the novel and the commercial film are both
narrative forms; that film inevitably follows the
novel in the presentation and affirmation of human-
istic values, especially of the triumph of man over
machine[4] and of the recovery and representation for
the viewer of a previously lost, unmediated reality;[5]
and that the film is essentially just another branch
of literature.[6]

All of these clichés, like most clichés, contain
some elements of truth, but that truth is worn away
by overuse, obscured by metaphysical baggage, and
confused by an essentialism that regards both film
and novel as single, ahistorical, ideal entities.
Moreover, as Charles Eidsvik has pointed out, "film"
the medium--the strip of celluloid running through
the projector--is usually confused "with its dominant genre, the narrative."[7] (Unfortunately, Eidsvik
himself goes on to confuse literature with the medium
of print.) It should be clear enough by now that the
novel and the narrative film are indeed both means
of telling stories, but that they also both have histories and are in turn grounded in history, particularly the histories of the American and European middle classes.

Within narrative forms, as Christian Metz and
Jonathan Culler have both reminded us, there is a
system of codes and conventions--what we might call

"literature" in general and what Metz specifically
labels as "cinema"--and the <u>working</u> of codes in
texts--the individual novel or film.[8] Seeing the
two narrative forms as analogous--that is, that
"cinema" as a set of codes and conventions is to literature as the individual film is to the novel--we
should be able to intelligently apply what the
screenwriters have always told us--that a novel must
be translated to the screen in cinematic terms. I
say "intelligently apply" because the problems and
motivations of translation from one medium to another
are far more complex than even the translation of
poetry from one language to another. The conventions
and codes of narrative film do derive much--as
Eisenstein told us--from those of the novel.[9] Yet
they also derive from many other sources in theater,
art, photography and mass culture, as we have learned
from Erwin Panofsky, John Fell, and Keith Cohen.[10]
With this wealth of resources incorporated in the
narrative codes of film, there is no reason that any
novel should be impoverished by its translation from
page to screen.

Such impoverishment does occur, though, and is
more often than not expected. The reason it occurs
and the reason why (though we expect it) we are continually disappointed is that both literary and
filmic texts are grounded in and part of daily social
practice. Both adaptors and spectators have certain
assumptions about adaptations which derive from their
places in time and society and which are not always
directed toward the same goals. A text has its birth
in relation to its time and retains at least vestiges
of that meaning, but its meanings and its significance beyond the page or screen change along with the
society beyond the page or screen. In turn, in the
adaptation of any novel into film, these changes are
inevitably manifested within three broad areas. One
of these is the historical matrix within which the
text has its origin, its popular reception, its critical study, and its conversion to film. Another is
the aesthetic intent of the adaptor in conjunction
with market pressures to produce a saleable commodity.
Finally there are ideological constraints, both covert, manifested in sociological and psychological
subtexts, and overt, resulting from direct pressures
to bring a text into conformity with dominant moral
and political practices.

Of course, these classifications are an over-
simplification since all three areas are inseparably
intertwined, often overlapping and sometimes con-
gruent; still, they provide a set of guidelines by
which to begin a measure of the process of adaptation. In providing keys to understanding the motivations, possibly conflicting, which underlie various adaptations, we should be able to read the process of transformation as well as the texts being
transformed.

The historical matrix of any given novel affects
how it is read and changed by its adaptor(s) in two
ways. First, any reading is affected by time and by
the changes that any reader brings to a text. Professional literary historians have problems enough
in trying to reproduce an accurate reading of a
work according to its origin in history, so the problem is even more acute for the reader who comes to
the work without scholarly knowledge or a professional air of detachment (if, in fact, such knowledge is ever complete and true or such detachment
completely possible). We do not have to agree completely with Harold Bloom and insist that all readings are misreadings, to recognize that one's personal, lived experience as well as those dislocations of modern consciousness represented by evolution, Marxism, depth psychology, relativity, and
feminism have changed and continue to change (to
varying degrees, of course) the ways in which we
look at novels produced before these dislocations.
This intellectual "distortion" is greater the more
distant culturally and historically the adaptor is
from his or her source. Thus, although Martin C.
Battestin generally praises the adaptation of Tom
Jones by John Osborne and Tony Richardson, he does
conclude that the film lacks Fielding's moral vision
--necessarily so, because a modern mass audience
will not share the same attitudes and beliefs which
Fielding could assume in his readers. As a more modern instance, no present-day filmmaker could share
the naiveté of D. W. Griffith in believing that
bringing Thomas Dixon's The Clansman to the screen
as Birth of a Nation was not a racist act.
Second, the degree of historical distortion in
an adaptation is complicated further by the cultural
history of the novel. Only rarely does a well-known

work escape a popularization which incorporates the
text as a part of general mass culture with little
or no regard for its actual content. In these cases,
the text which is brought to the screen is less the
novel itself than the novel as bowdlerized for public school texts, as fitted out for touring stage
presentations, as enshrined in lovable characters
(and even lovable authors) from the canons of Acceptable Literature. This enshrinement in the classic
Hollywood film is perhaps most obvious in those films
which open with the cover, title page, and perhaps
opening page of the book itself. This device functions to assure the spectator that the movie is a
"faithful" adaptation of the novel (whether it is or
not). Of course, the same device was often used in
adaptations of contemporary best sellers as well; in
either case, the audience is being promised the pres-
tige of the novel. Gregory Ratoff's 1949 Black Magic
goes one step further. The film opens with a con-
versation in which Alexandre Dumas's père complains
to his son (appropriately referred to as the author
of Camille) about the block he is having in writing
about the magician-hypnotist Cagliostro. As the
author begins to recount the details of Cagliostro's
career, there is a dissolve into the main narrative
of the film which itself concludes with a dissolve
to a hand, writing: "The End. Alexandre Dumas." A
bit of black magic has also taken place here. A
verbal recounting of a story has given way to its
dramatic representation which has in turn become the
novel itself, all sanctified by the seeming physical
presence of one of the great Romantic storytellers.
     Canonization of the text within the realm of
mass culture helps to explain the scandalous adaptations so many works have had. Nowhere is this more
apparent than in the treatment of those dark and subversive works which have been cleaned up and banished
to the realm of Children's Literature--notably,
Gulliver's Travels, Huckleberry Finn, and Alice in
Wonderland. Norman Z. McLeod's 1933 version of
Alice, for example, is wonderfully cast but literally
enshrines its subject by making all the actors wear
masks modeled after the Tenniel drawings. (The
Disney version has more to do with Mickey Mouse than
Lewis Carroll.) Clearly, works which raise funda-
mental questions about the nature of humanity (like
Gulliver), about duty to a personal moral vision

over social moral conventions (as in <u>Huckleberry
Finn</u>), and about the logic and justice of education
and authority (as in <u>Alice</u>) will very rarely find
full expression in a centralized, industrialized mass
medium. This, though, is the realm of ideology,
which is yet to be discussed.

Aesthetic considerations in adaptations may be
the most difficult to deal with, though they seem
the simplest. It is the aesthetic response of the
individual filmmaker to the novel which is usually
found wanting by the weekly popular movie reviewers,
and it is either the failure of that response or the
technical obstacles to a satisfactory adaptation
that are the focus for so many discussions of adaptations. What makes the aesthetic actually so difficult to deal with, though, is not just the problem
of knowing the personal and subjective response of
an adaptor to a novel, but the fact that that response is itself incorporated in the historical matrix of the novel and bound up in ideology. For the
moment, however, we can isolate three varieties of
response by the adaptor to the text: first, a desire
to "reproduce" the text, to bring the novel to the
screen--what is usually called a "faithful" adaptation; second, a more or less significant alteration
to the work to fit the adaptor's own artistic purposes; and finally, a conscious effort to criticize,
subvert, undercut or deconstruct the novel itself,
even to the point of altering it entirely. All
three responses may themselves spring from a variety
of motivations--some even at odds with each other--
and none of these responses guarantees that the completed adaptation will be adequate to the response.
The reason for the different motivations underlying these aesthetic responses has to do with the
perennial question of film authorship. Most basi-
cally, it is the writer who is responsible for transforming the novel into the screenplay, but we are all
aware of the transformations which even a screenplay
can undergo in filming. The director is most often
responsible for the final product, but in a
Hollywood-type system, final responsibility may be
removed from the director and assigned to a studio
editor or may even be relegated to the producer. The
problem is obvious enough, but I mention it once more
just to draw attention to the fact that the process

of adaptation can rarely be neatly held to a uniform
set of circumstances, the simple fusion of two con-
sciousnesses resulting in a final product. Even
though, for the sake of time and space, I will refer
mainly to the "adaptor" without specifying a specific
role for that individual, we must be aware that the
dialectics of film and print are considerably more
complicated.

The "faithful" adaptation is probably the one
most desired and demanded by the popular critics,
the one we think of as being the ideal adaptation,
but immediately a question arises: "Faithful to
what?" Like the Law, novels are said to have a
"letter" and a "spirit," and it is considered better
to be faithful to the spirit than to engage in a
"slavish" following of the original text. The
"spirit" of the novel, though, is precisely what
changes in the historical matrix within which we
read the novel. Some works simply cannot be read
completely in their original "spirit"--if, in fact,
that entity can ever be isolated--and not only because we misread but also because an "accurate" reading would be intolerable.

Faithfulness to the "letter" of the novel seems
easier; seemingly, all one has to do is reproduce the
characters, the events and the dialogue, but we have
all seen enough movies to know that is not sufficient
either. First, there are the constraints of time and
money within commercial exhibition practices. Few
adaptations can completely cover a work in the time
of a feature-length film and few producers are willing or able to put up enough money to finance a complete adaptation (though the occasional successes of
television mini-series like Shogun may change this
practice). Secondly, faithfulness to the "letter"
may be impossible because it is the letter. Those
adaptations which have been judged most disappointing
are usually of works in which language and narrative
technique are heavily foregrounded. Unless the cinematic narrative and image are foregrounded in similar
ways, unless cinematic tropes are substituted for
literary ones, the result is Martin Ritt's The Sound
and the Fury, from which the play of consciousness in
Benjy, Quentin, and Jason has disappeared; or Paul
Newman's Sometimes a Great Notion, which straightens
Ken Kesey's revelatory, insistent, continually loop-
ing, multi-voiced narration into just another family

saga; or Joseph Strick's <u>Ulysses</u>, which becomes, as
Pauline Kael puts it, "readings from the book plus
illustrated slides."[11]

To ask, "Faithful to <u>what?</u>" also requires a recognition that most adaptations are made to assure a
profit. It was not simply an innate desire by early
filmmakers to bring favorite stories to life that
prompted them to adapt novels, short stories and
plays for the screen; it was also the need for a
product. Once it was discovered that stories on
film drew audiences, there arose a need for more and
more stories to consume. Novel rights are bought by
producers not from love of literature, but because
a successful or prestigious book can assure a good
return, and if the work in question is a classic in
the public domain, so much the better. In addition,
submitting a work to the rationalizing and conven-
tionalizing processes of mass culture usually over-
rides any question of faithfulness to a text. Adaptors and producers who see the novel as a consumable
product, who envision <u>Crime</u> <u>and</u> <u>Punishment</u> as a swell
detective story, are legendary in the folklore of
Hollywood.

Even in Hollywood, though, there are exceptions,
and there have been and are filmmakers whose avowed
purpose was or is to bring the novel to the screen
in a completely faithful production. But still the
question asserts itself: "Faithful to <u>what?</u>" Eric
von Stroheim, David O. Selznick, and Robert Bresson
all claimed utter fidelity to the text when they
made, respectively, <u>Greed</u>, <u>Gone</u> <u>with</u> <u>the</u> <u>Wind</u>, and
<u>Diary</u> <u>of</u> <u>a</u> <u>Country</u> <u>Priest</u>. Each is a very different
book, adapted for very different reasons, resulting
in very different films. Even when an adaptation is
successful in conveying a book to screen, we are
still obligated to examine the source and motivations
of that adaptation, to ask for what purpose this film
was made. Stroheim's insistent naturalism,
Selznick's apotheosis of Hollywood style, and the
elliptical quietness of Bresson cannot be equated
simply because each adaptation is "faithful." A
simple-minded notion of faithfulness, whether to
letter or spirit, only serves to obscure the works
and the process and remove them from history while
isolating them from ideology.

A second response by filmmakers to individual
texts is to make the work faithful to <u>themselves</u>, to

recast it and adapt it to conform to their own ob-
sessions and personal visions. Obviously, this form
of adaptation is employed most fully by those directors whose identifiable body of works and continuing
themes and concerns label them as auteurs. With The
Grapes of Wrath, for example, Nunally Johnson and
John Ford transform John Steinbeck's nascent social-
ism into a nostalgic populism typical of Ford's other
films.[12] Orson Welles in The Magnificent Amerbersons,
The Trial, and The Immortal Story, is at least as
much concerned with his own continuing depiction of
the results of lost innocence, of personal corrup-
tion, and of the redemptive powers of story-telling
as with an accurate depiction of the individual
worlds of Booth Tarkington, Franz Kafka, and Isak
Dinesen. The adaptor's vision may be as much a
sociological one as an artistic one. Taking Richard
Brooks's postwar novel, The Brick Foxhole--a badly
confused expression of antimilitarism and psychological and sexual insecurity--Dore Schary and Edward
Dmytryk fashioned the film Crossfire--a tightly constructed thriller which attacks anti-Semitism and
makes an overt left-liberal appeal for social justice. Babette Mangolte, in her production of Henry
James's What Maisie Knew, literally reshapes the text
to her--in fact, the camera's--vision. Discarding
most of any plot (not just James's) and setting the
film in a contemporary urban apartment, Mangolte uses
a subjective camera to recreate a child's vision
while bringing the viewer's vision into question at
the same time. Again, there is a wide divergence of
motives and means in adapting novels. Filmmakers
who reform the work to their own desires are certainly not offering faithful adaptations, but such adaptations would likely be less powerful and coherent
if they did not reform to answer new questions and to
fit into a new context.

      That context may sometimes be a questioning, un-
dermining, or deconstruction of the original novel
itself. Mangolte's Maisie certainly points in that
direction, as does the production of Sigmund Freud's
Dora by Anthony McCall, Claire Pajaczkowska, Andrew
Tyndall, and Jane Weinstock. Though Dora is not a
traditional literary text, the film uses Freud's
account of his patient to demonstrate how he himself
in fact did read her as a text and subverts that
reading by placing the narrative of the original in

a variety of visual and narrative contexts which un-
dermine Freud's own reading and open up new questions. Novels may have been undermined by Hollywood
adaptors for their own, mostly commercial purposes,
but that process is an obscuring and covering of the
original text. The radical filmmaker, on the other
hand, wishes to undercut the novel in order to expose
its underlying assumptions and basic premises, often
to substitute new assumptions in a radical rereading
of the text. Keith Cohen has shown how Sergei
Eisenstein tried to do precisely this in his plans
to adapt Theodore Dreiser's An American Tragedy.
Taking an already radical American novel, Eisenstein
intended to probe even deeper and offer a truly
Marxist analysis of the capitalist class relationships in the novel. It almost goes without saying
that Eisenstein's version was never filmed; the project instead went to that arch-aesthete, Joseph von
Sternberg. Cohen, though, holds up Eisenstein's project as a model for all adaptations and makes a con-
vincing case for the necessity of a sense of purpose
beyond the mere adaptation itself: "The adaptation
must subvert its original, perform a double and para-
doxical job of masking and unveiling its source, or
else the pleasure it provides will be nothing more
than that of seeing words changed into images."[13]
     Such a conception and such a project of adapta-
tion was perhaps impossible in the classic Hollywood
era, but one place in which research is needed is
the determination of whether it was in fact impossible. So much has been said about inadequacies in
Hollywood's approach to novels that we may be over-
looking cases in which the adaptation did in fact go
beneath and beyond the text. Such films certainly
were possible by the 1950s, even if they were not
performed with the rigor and purpose an Eisenstein
might bring to them. Genre films may be most prone
to such textual rereadings; certainly, two prime
examples have come from the realm of the detective
film. Robert Aldrich's Kiss Me Deadly is completely
different in attitude from a more traditional version of Mickey Spillane like Victor Saville's I, the
Jury. In the Aldrich film, Mike Hammer is exposed
as a thoroughly contemptible creature--a bully, liar,
blackmailer, and petty sadist whose greed leads to
the detonation of an atomic bomb and his own destruc-
tion. On a somewhat more subtle level, Robert

Altman's The Long Goodbye outraged Raymond Chandler
fans by the transformation of Philip Marlowe,
Chandler's knight of chivalry patrolling the mean
streets of modern society, into an anachronism in
the sensual, high-tech world of 1970s Los Angeles--
such an anachronism that he finally forgets his personal code of honor and stoops to murder and revenge.

   This last category of aesthetic response to the
printed text--the subversion or undermining of the
text--leads naturally into our final area of concern,
that of ideological constraints. A conscious ideological purpose like that of Eisenstein has the
special virtue of providing a solid theoretical
framework within which to adapt a work, but when the
ideology in question is that of the dominant society
within which the adaptation is made--the capitalist,
bourgeois society which founded and sustained
Hollywood--conscious ideology disappears or seems to.
Here we are in the realm of ideology as redefined by
Louis Althusser, as the way in which people live the
relationship between themselves and the conditions
of their existence.[14] Ideology, then, is the con-
tinual procession of daily events which confirms and
naturalizes all human relations. Obviously, cultural
media play an extremely important role in such natu-
ralization. The upper middle class is elevated and
displayed as the norm; sexual relationships are
placed within a patriarchal framework with little or
no question paid to the place of woman; the individual is always given priority and ascendence over the
group.
   When both novels and films are produced within
ideology, without self-awareness, then they usually
unquestioningly reproduce that ideology and it is
the task of the reader or spectator alone to under-
mine these texts by concentrating on the contradic-
tions, gaps, and fissures that inevitably occur
within the narrative. Of course, the historical matrix is in process here too. A change in lived relationships produces changed perceptions and changed
readings. Films like Stella Dallas and Mildred
Pierce insist even more forcefully than the novels
from which they came that women who seek personal
satisfaction and financial success over duty and
subservience to a man will lose everything (including themselves in the form of their adored daugh-

ters), but fewer people today than ever before are
willing to accept such a covert message and more can
recognize it as a message. The ideology of the text
eventually loses its invisibility and stands exposed,
even though it is replaced by new ideologies and new
forms of ideology.

A separate, though related, problem is that of
the ideology of the image. Much of the important
film scholarship of the last decade has called into
question and examined the nature of the film image,
especially its claimed ability to reproduce or represent reality. Noting the origins of the movie
camera in the camera obscura which ordered and ra-
tionalized vision in painting for the rising middle
classes of the Renaissance, critics associated with
the Cahiers du cinéma in France and the British
journal Screen have seen the function of the film
image as the placement and even construction of an
individual, seemingly autonomous spectator-subject.
The critique of this film image has begun, both by
critics and by filmmakers, but what is also needed
is an examination of the ideology of the film image
in adaptations in relation to the ideology of the
real which is subsumed within the texts from which
the films derive. Such a project can only be suggested here, but it is one more item for future film
study.

Finally, we must remember that ideology also
functions overtly, censoring and editing in the name
of moral, economic, and political righteousness. The
Hays Office and the Production Code were the most obvious manifestations of this sort of control, but
even they are too often forgotten as we look at the
shape a novel took in making its way to the screen.
Less obvious, and needing a more detailed history,
are direct interventions in movies for political reasons, such as that which Constance Pohl has detailed
in regard to For Whom the Bell Tolls.[15] As Gerald
· Peary and Roger Shatzkin remind us, ideology can be
quite conscious as well as unconscious, and it is one
of the duties of scholars and critics to deal with
the interrelationships of both and to recognize their
functioning.[16]

These brief remarks can only begin to detail the
work which needs to be done in the study of adaptations. In separating the historical matrix, the

adaptor's individual response, and the ideological
constraints upon the adaptation, I have just hinted
at the complexity of the ways in which these cate-
gories affect each other. I have not discussed
their relationship to technology, though this must
eventually be addressed, and I have been able to
offer only a few tentative examples of these various
areas. I have not offered a history or a theory;
instead, I have offered some directions and considerations which must be addressed if the history and
theory of adaptations are to proceed. Drama and
poetry (and the essay as well) will eventually have
to come under similar consideration. Recent works
like Keith Cohen's Film and Fiction and anthologies
like those of Peary and Shatzkin point the way to
future study. We also need a further awareness of
alternative cinematic practices in the American and
European avant-garde, in foreign cinemas like that
of prewar Japan, and in the emerging filmmakers of
the third world.
     To study the process of adaptation is to under-
take several things at once: a consideration of the
nature of narrative art, a theoretical view of high
and popular culture, a history of the commerce of
images and narratives. We do need to understand
what makes an adaptation effective--the concern of
most writing on adaptation so far--but that effectiveness itself is a far less tangible entity than
is at first apparent. As mass culture ever more
voraciously seeks out images and narratives for pro-
cessing and consumption, adaptation will become increasingly important. The text will lose its boundaries as it shifts from book to movie to television
series to comic book to novelization in serial form.
To understand the future, which is already with us,
we must understand the past and present, and we must
see how we ourselves may become the texts unless we
are aware.

                         NOTES

[1]Charles Eidsvik, "Toward a 'Politique des
Adaptations,'" in Film and/as Literature, ed. John

Harrington (Englewood Cliffs, N.J.: Prentice-Hall, 1977), pp. 27-37.

[2]Edward Murray, The Cinematic Imagination: Writers and the Motion Pictures (New York: Frederick Ungar, 1972), p. 292.

[3]George Bluestone, Novels into Film (Baltimore: The Johns Hopkins Press, 1957), p. 5.

[4]Robert Richardson, Literature and Film (Bloomington: University of Indiana Press, 1969).

[5]Andre Bazin, "The Ontology of the Photographic Image," in What is Cinema? (Berkeley: University of California Press, 1967), pp. 9-16; Sigfried Kracauer, Theory of Film: The Redemption of Physical Reality (New York: Oxford Press, 1960); Frank D. McConnell, The Spoken Seen (Baltimore: John Hopkins University Press, 1975).

[6]See Harrington, also Maurice Beja, Film and Literature (New York: Longwood, 1979).

[7]Eidsvik, "The Art of Literature, the Medium of Film," in Harrington, p. 306.

[8]Christian Metz, Language and Cinema, trans. Donna Jean Umiker Sebeok (The Hague: Mouton, 1974), especially pp. 285-286; Jonathan Culler, Structuralist Poetics (Ithaca, N.Y.: Cornell University Press, 1975), p. 116.

[9]Sergei Eisenstein, "Dickens, Griffith, and the Film Today," Film Form, trans. Jay Leyda (New York: Harcourt, Brace and World, 1949), pp. 195-255.

[10]Erwin Panofsky, "Style and Medium in the Motion Pictures," Critique 1 (Jan.-Feb. 1947); John L. Fell, Film and the Narrative Tradition (Norman: University of Oklahoma Press, 1974); Keith Cohen, Film and Fiction: The Dynamics of Exchange (New Haven: Yale University Press, 1979).

[11]Pauline Kael, Kiss Kiss Bang Bang (New York: Bantam, 1969), p. 206.

[12]For a more complete discussion of this adaptation, see Russell Campbell, "Trampling Out the Vintage: Sour Grapes," The Modern American Novel and the Movies, ed. Gerald Peary and Roger Shatzkin (New York: Frederick Ungar, 1978), pp. 107-118.

[13]Cohen, "Eisenstein's Subversive Adaptation,"
The Classic American Novel and the Movies, ed. Gerald
Peary and Roger Shatzkin (New York: Frederick Ungar,
1977), p. 255.

[14]Louis Althusser, "Marxism and Humanism," For
Marx, cited by John Ellis, "Introduction," Screen
Reader 1 (London: Society for Education in Film and
Television, 1977), p. x.

[15]Constance Pohl, "The 'Unmaking' of a Political
Film," The Modern American Novel and the Movies,
pp. 317-324.

9

THE BIBLE INTO FILM: "BRING ON THE
DANCING GIRLS" OR, "THROW
THEM TO THE LIONS, SIRE"

Katherine B. Pavlik

Someone once defined the historical film as one
in which "people write with feathers." He might also
have included movies in which people write on papy-
rus. Some of the earliest historical films were
based on biblical sources, including D. W. Griffith's
epics Judith of Bethulia (1913) taken from a story in
the Apocrypha and Intolerance (1916), one segment of
which dealt with the life of Christ. Versions of
Salome and Samson and Delilah appeared in 1918 and
1922 and Cecil B. DeMille included a prologue about
Moses in his 1923 The Ten Commandments (actually a
modern story). The life of Jesus appeared on film
very early: among others, a three-reel Life of Christ
(1908); Edison's Star of Bethlehem (1909); and the
first major Life in 1912, Sidney Olcott's From the
Manger to the Cross. Filmmakers also turned to religious historical novels and plays which had been
loosely adapted from biblical and other historical
writings. The first of these "Lions and Christians"
epics were Ben Hur (1908), Quo Vadis (1912), and The
Sign of the Cross (1914). Since these early days,
filmmakers have produced hundreds of films based on
the Old and New Testament, some of them the biggest
money-makers of all time.

Although these films <u>have</u> been immensely popular
and lucrative, few films based on the Bible have
achieved critical acclaim. Recent efforts have been
treated mostly with scorn by film scholars, who cite
difficulties with the epic genre in general, and with
biblical sources in particular. These difficulties
exist whether the story is adapted directly from
scripture or derived indirectly from a historical
novel. Indeed, when examining a number of these
films it is clear that there <u>are</u> special problems
with putting Bible stories on film, problems which
don't always occur with other period dramas adapted
from literature.

First, most films based on the Bible are of the
epic genre; they last longer than ordinary films,
employ "casts of thousands," and attempt to give the
sweep and scope of the period. Rudolf Arnheim suggests that the epic mode generally does not adapt
well to film (D. W. Griffith notwithstanding).
Arnheim points out that the epic is not concerned
with change and the solution to a problem, but with
<u>describing</u> invariable [human] existence. It is es-
sentially a static mode concerned, as Goethe said,
"[with] man as he acts outwardly; battle, travels,
any kind of enterprise that requires some sensuous
breadth."[1]

Thus, because of their descriptive nature, epic
films often lack a suspenseful, dynamic plot, pro-
ceeding from step to step to a climax, as we find in
dramatic films. Despite their efforts at visual excitement, epic films are often static and boring.
Episodes are strung together in sequence and sometimes seem merely a pretext for showing more sumptu-
ous palaces and dancing girls. Because of this episodic nature, epic films also lack involving character development; characters appear flat and stero-
typed, perhaps because they represent either the human condition or some general type of that historical
era. Finally, since epics often deal with history
spread over long periods of time, they include <u>many</u>
characters instead of the few we involve ourselves
with in dramatic films.

In addition to these general problems with adapting the epic genre, biblical stories have certain
built-in problems in both content and style, which
prevent them from being effective on film. In discussing these problems I will divide biblical films

into four somewhat artificial subgenres: early-
Christian epics adapted from historical novels; epics
directly adapted from the Old Testament; and epics on
the life of Christ. This third category is the most
numerous and presents special problems. A fourth
type of biblical film takes a low-key, realistic approach, avoids spectacle, and instead stresses the
simple values and moral power of the scripture.
    Although Bible stories appear to present fas-
cinating possibilities for novels and films, they
don't offer much detail or plot on which to hang a
feature film or long novel. The answer is to include many subplots, fictional characters (especially
a love/sex interest), action (often not found in the
original story), and much period detail, one reason
why people have always liked historical novels.
Three novels partially based on biblical sources,
Ben Hur by Lew Wallace, Quo Vadis by the Polish
writer, Henryk Sienkiewicz, and The Robe by Lloyd C.
Douglas, use just these techniques to tell the story
of early Christianity, and so do the films based on
the novels. The plots of these films (and of many
others like them) are so amazingly similar that they
could be called the "Throw them to the lions, sire,"
genre.
    Based on the years immediately following the
crucifixion, these films deal with the spread of
Christianity throughout the Roman world. Scriptural
sources for this period are few--a few references in
the Acts of the Apostles and Paul's Epistles. More
relevant are the writings of the Roman historian,
Tacitus. Each film/novel concerns a nonbeliever (in
Quo Vadis and The Robe he is a highborn Roman; in
Ben Hur he is an aristocratic Jew) who first perse-
cutes or scorns the Christians and then is converted,
sometimes because of the efforts of a pure, lovely
Christian maiden. In The Robe, the protagonist con-
verts the girl! In some films, there is a "bad" girl
in the form of a sexy pagan princess who attempts to
lure the new Christian to the fleshpots of the deca-
dent Roman civilization.
    All these films stress the opulence, brutality,
and decadence of the Romans. Sets are lavish, and
in recent versions, colorful. To emphasize the theme
of decadence and cruelty, Roman emperors are fiends
(I'll never forget Peter Ustinov as Nero in the 1951
version of Quo Vadis, fiddling while Rome burned),

and most aristocratic Romans are debauched. Quo
Vadis especially dwells on the sufferings of the
Christians in the arena where they are tossed to the
lions and burned en masse. All of this on the wide
screen comes across more vividly than in the novels,
whose style is somewhat turgid, as befitting the
religiosity of the subject.

These films illustrate in exaggerated form the
difficulties in basing films (and novels) on limited
biblical sources, or, in fact, on ancient history in
general. Since the Bible contains so little informa-
tion about early Christianity, and Tacitus little
more, the director must create characters and situations to fill the immensities of time. For example,
in The Robe Marcellus, the young Roman, is converted
to Christianity halfway through the film and obviously must die for his beliefs. But, because there is
much time to fill, Henry Koster obliges with many
irrelevant action sequences including a drawn out
escape from a Roman dungeon. In Ben Hur, the religious theme takes a back seat to the chariot race,
the most memorable scene in both film versions (1926/
1959). Unfortunately, this emphasis on spectacle and
action obscures the theme of the goodness and simplicity of the Christians contrasted with the Romans.

This problem of "thin content" and resultant com-
pensating "sound and fury" is also a problem in films
adapted directly from biblical sources. The story of
Moses and the Exodus is one of the most detailed in
the Bible, taking up much of Exodus and parts of
Leviticus, Numbers, and Deuteronomy, and yet the sec-
tions dealing directly with Moses and his doings are
fragmentary and brief. Moses is characterized almost
entirely by his actions and only slightly by speech,
as are most people in the Old Testament. Our interest is not so much in the gripping but relatively
brief conflict between Moses and the Pharaoh as it
is in the more abstract moral significance of a people freed by a great leader. Secondary characters
in the tale, such as Moses' wife and his brother,
Aaron, are not characterized at all.

To the bare bones of this story, then, a director
must weld more content to fill a long film. Cecil B.
DeMille in The Ten Commandments (1956) fills these
thin spots with much speculation about Moses' childhood and youth, a ridiculous love interest with an
evil Egyptian princess (never hinted at in the

Bible), many crowd scenes, and special effects.
There is no doubt that DeMille is partially successful in rendering the epic sense of a whole people
stirred and on the move. The spectacle in the film
is impressive, especially the long shots of the Jews
toiling on the pyramids and moving out of Egypt into
the Sinai. However, as one critic said in her initial review: "Bustle gives this picture some vital-
ity, but mere busyness is not enough."[2] Even the
special effects such as the parting of the Red Sea
and the killing of the firstborn seem weak. Because
DeMille concentrates on these outwardly exciting,
child-like aspects, he loses touch with the moral
power of the story of the Exodus. Also, a lack of
narrative structure in the original tale shows
through the film; it is episodic and sags badly after
the Exodus, and the last section detailing the wan-
derings in the desert seems almost an afterthought.

DeMille's Samson and Delilah (1949), adapted from
a brief episode in Judges, suffers from the same
ills. DeMille takes a simple story of love and be-
trayal and builds it into an epic filled with "more
chariots, more peacock plumes, more animals, more
beards, and more sex than ever before."[3] Since
Judges does not tell us why Delilah betrays Samson
to the Philistines (other than for eleven hundred
pieces of silver, not a very romantic reason),
DeMille uses an elaborate subplot to explain this;
he also has a repentant Delilah visit the blinded,
captive Samson. She is almost demure, completely
changed from the seductress she portrays in the beginning of the film. Surely the author of Judges
would blanch, since one of the points of the story
is to expose the evils of foreign women. In his
autobiography, DeMille defends himself: "All I did
was find the thread that tied the narrative of
Samson's life together. . . . I am sometimes accused
of gingering up the Bible with large and lavish in-
fusions of sex and violence. I can only wonder if
my accusers have ever read certain parts of the
Bible."[4] Although sex is certainly present in Samson
and Delilah, it is understated, as is always the case
in the Bible. Unfortunately, understatement of sex
isn't good box office.

Another problem in DeMille's epics, as well as
in other biblical films, is the tendency to use well
known actors in all parts. This may be good box

office, but leads to the sport of "actor spotting,"
rather than following the story.[5] Further, since the
Bible doesn't describe people physically, we each
have our mental images of what Moses, the Pharaoh,
and Samson and Delilah looked like. When we see
Charlton Heston, Yul Brynner, Victor Mature, and Hedy
Lamarr in these roles, it is a bit distracting.
DeMille explained he chose Mature and Lamarr since
they represented for him "the essence of maleness and
femininity," but to others they epitomize the essence
of Hollywood. In general, it seems the directors of
historical films would do better to choose relatively
unknown actors, whether or not we know what the character looked like.

Perhaps the most ambitious undertaking of a biblical film project to date (not including John
Heyman's project to be discussed later) is John
Huston's The Bible (1966), which actually covers only
the Creation and parts of the tales of the patri-
archs. The Bible is a huge and sprawling epic, intended to overwhelm the senses--"gigantic myth-
making."[6] Huston avoids the lavish sets of DeMille,
showing the Hebrew people as they were--simple no-
mads. The Creation sequences are quite beautiful,
showing rolling mists parting to reveal new forests,
waters, and mountains. Fields of running and grazing
animals introduce us to the new creatures. Shots of
volcanos erupting give a sense of a world in the
making. The acting is strong, with special praise
going to George C. Scott, one well-known face who can
move with credibility into varied roles. As Abraham,
Scott manages to convey both the anguish of a father
forced to sacrifice his only son, and the awe and
humility of a man bowing to the will of Jehovah.

Somehow, however, it doesn't work. There is no
central focus (in fact, no plot in the conventional
sense) to unify the various episodes, except for the
sonorous voice of Huston as the Lord reading passages
from the scripture. Huston doesn't know what to do
with Adam and Eve's nakedness: they hop from conven-
ient bush to bush until it becomes humorous. A
folksy Huston himself plays Noah, cajoling a recal-
citrant turtle up the gangplank. No doubt he means
to humanize Noah, but the power and awe of the wrath
of God found in the Old Testament is missing. Like
DeMille, Huston fails to communicate the spirit of
these ancient writings to twentieth-century audiences.

When a director attempts a biblical film on a nonepic scale, when he "sticks to the text," in order to give a true picture of the culture, the results can be disappointing. In David and Bathsheba (1952) Henry King tells the story of King David's love for Bathsheba, the wife of one of his soldiers, in a straightforward, unadorned fashion. Since ninth-century B.C. Hebrews were a culturally backward people (in the sense of wealth and technology), David's palace is quite plain, dancing girls are not much in evidence, and the Hebrew troops' armor and weapons are simple. The story concentrates on the David-Bathsheba episode, although it does make one concession to excitement with a flashback to the Goliath legend. Goliath appears as a mighty big man, but not a monster, as DeMille might have made him.

Again, it doesn't come off. The film is stilted, dull, and too plain, with little to replace the spectacle of DeMille. Because it would have involved a much longer, more elaborate film, the story ignores the later problems that resulted from David's affair with Bathsheba (his old age struggles with his sons by different wives). If the viewer is familiar with II Samuel and I Kings, this can be disturbing. Also, dialogue is again weak; people in the Old Testament speak little, and when Susan Hayward as Bathsheba says to David, "When we break the law of Moses we should at least know what we are doing," the reader of Samuel stirs uncomfortably in his seat. It seems that nobody, whether novelist or script writer, has been able to figure out how people in the ancient world actually talked to each other. Gregory Peck makes a solemn, down-to-earth David, but maybe his face is too well known to accept as the King of Israel and Judah.

Films on the life of Christ comprise at least half of the films based on biblical sources. Here the filmmaker has much more written material (the four Gospels), yet by and large these films suffer from the same defects as Old Testament films. The first really "big" version of Christ's life was DeMille's King of Kings (1927); highly praised by contemporary critics, it still remains one of the few films about Christ that has received critical acclaim. The making of this film is instructive about the inherent difficulties of the subject. How does one render on the screen a character whom many in the

audience believe to be the living God? In Old Testament films, God is a felt presence, seen in the action of the elements, or a voice ("I am that I am,"
speaks the burning bush in The Ten Commandments).
God made Man is something else.

DeMille saw this problem and countered it by
choosing H. B. Warner to play Christ; Warner was a
"manly man," according to DeMille, and wouldn't play
a sanctimonious, effeminate Christ, something he saw
as a definite danger. To avoid the shock of an initial sharp image of Christ's face, he shows the face
slowly coming into focus in the eyes of a blind girl
who has just been made to see. Contemporary critics
agreed that this was a moving, effective device.
King of Kings made a tremendous impression on audiences and critics; however, there were problems with
the interpretation of Christ and with the film as a
whole. Some critics felt the film was too literal
and dwelt overly long on the crucifixion, while
others felt H. B. Warner's performance was too un-
earthly and failed to communicate Christ's humanity.
The New York Times reviewer hit on a major difficulty: "the presence of Jesus on the screen creates
a feeling akin to resentment largely because Mr.
DeMille has insisted on having his camera too close
to the player."8 The Old Testament taboo of not
looking at the "face" of God (Exodus 33:21-23) dies
hard.

Subsequent films about Jesus have faced the same
problems and others. King of Kings, remade in 1961
by Nicolas Ray, was criticized for the casting of
Jeffrey Hunter as Jesus, a bland, too young portrayal
which earned the film the name "I Was a Teenage
Jesus" in the trade. Trying to avoid a too well-
known actor, Ray made the greater mistake of using
an incompetent. George Stevens's 1965 The Greatest
Story Ever Told was lambasted for irrelevant subplots
about Barabas and a fictional Jewish rebellion
against the Romans, obviously concocted to make the
film relevant in the 1960s, and for dwelling too long
on Salome and John the Baptist, titilating and then
rewarding the audience with a close-up of the head on
a platter. Both these films use heavenly choirs,
pretty pastel colors, halo effects, and clumsily created close-up scenes with phony painted backdrops.
Says Stanley Kauffmann of The Greatest Story Ever
Told, ". . . the acting is generally adenoidal and

sententious. Most of the characters seem well aware
they are in The Greatest Story." Kauffmann does con-
gratulate Max Von Sydow for doing a competent job at
the "dreadful task of playing Jesus."[9]
     It is interesting to note how other directors
have dealt with Jesus. In films such as The Robe,
the 1926 version of Ben Hur, and The Big Fisherman
(1959), an early-Christian film, where Jesus appears
only a few times, we see him from afar, the back of
his head or hand, or the backs of the crosses on
Calvary. This is even more disconcerting than close-
ups. Of course, films which depict the Gospels must
show the face of Christ.
     One of the most realistic lives of Christ is
Paolo Pasolini's The Gospel According to St. Matthew
(1964). Pasolini, a Marxist, oddly combines a portrayal of Jesus as an angry young militant with a
stark, almost cinema verité approach straight from
Matthew. Shot in black and white in the stark, ra-
vaged landscape of southern Italy, the sets are exactly what one would expect first century Palestine
to look like. Even Herod's palace is slightly tacky.
The actors are all Italian peasants (except for Jesus
who is played by a young Spanish student); the faces
of the apostles are remarkably individualized, instead of the pleasant, brown bearded men in most
films. The music is also unique: a combination of
Bach, African songs, and American spirituals alter-
nates with silence. No celestial choirs here. Camera work is innovative; during the trial scene we
look on as a member of the crowd, peering over
Peter's shoulders.
     The film is full of stirring images: Joseph and
a very young, pregnant Mary struck with the knowledge
of the task they have been given; the infant Jesus
toddling toward Joseph's arms (here we see what "God
made Man" means); Jesus striding purposefully over a
wheat field, a man on a godly mission. Pasolini, an
atheist, does not shy away from the miracles (in some
films already mentioned they are performed off-
camera, or not performed at all); the cleansing of
the leper is done almost clumsily. We see his de-
formed face and Jesus reaching out to touch him.
Abruptly, the frame jumps and we see a perfect,
"clean" face. Yet, it does work. We feel a jolt and
pleasure for this inexplicable gift the leper has
been given. The Gospel consistently avoids clichés,

what Kauffmann calls the picturesque tableaux of the
famous scenes which make other films look like a cat-
alog of Christmas card scenes. The Last Supper is
shown, not as Leonardo's masterpiece, but as a group
of tired, discouraged men. We see the crucifixion,
not as a quiet repose, but as a horrible, degrading
death. In an interview Pasolini explained that he
wanted to avoid a "mere visualization" of the Gospels
--that his effort was first to communicate the
spirit, the mystery and power of the simple tales.[10]
The Gospel does do this and at the same time provides
a more realistic visualization than other films.

     For all these successes, though, the film has
serious weaknesses. For one, the total dependence
on Matthew leads to long soliloquies (the incanta-
tions to the scribes and pharisees), which seem to
have no relationship to prior or subsequent events.
In these interminable scenes we see Jesus' face in
close-up. Matthew might read well, but on film it
becomes heavy and static. Brendan Gill suggests
attendance at The Gospel for a Lenten penance, stating that the main problem is Pasolini's literal tran-
scription of Matthew; he feels the New Testament
leaves much to be desired as literature in construction and motivation. Gill states: ". . . if the old
method (DeMille) doesn't work, its opposite (The
Gospel) doesn't work, either."[11] Another problem is
the difficulty actors have in uttering convincingly
the words we have heard since childhood.

     As in other films, the portrayal of Jesus himself
is a weakness of The Gospel. Pasolini emphasizes
Jesus' ardent impatience with the hypocrites around
him. His tone becomes more and more ardent and finally righteous; he lacks the kindliness and warmth
we associate with Jesus. Even the Sermon on the
Mount comes across as a diatribe, not a loving hom-
ily. Pauline Kael calls him "a prissy, loathsome
young man," and says she couldn't wait for the crucifixion.[12] "Loathsome" is perhaps too strong, but
certainly I, too, became impatient for the ending.
Fortunately, films about Jesus do have a definite
ending; they don't stretch out to infinity like films
on the Old Testament.

     Films about Jesus accentuate a question raised by
any film treating a religious subject: just how does
one depict a supernatural event, a miracle? One approach is to not show it at all, the idea being that

modern audiences will not accept the supernatural
(horror is different because we know it's just a
story and suspend our disbelief); this approach, however, is a disappointment since we know the stories
and expect to see the miracles. Worse yet is to depict them poorly: I remember my incredulity at age
thirteen watching the Spirit of the Lord God seeping
like green slime under Pharaoh's door. The best approach is probably Pasolini's; the technique does not
have to be perfect if the director can communicate
the spirit or idea of the miracle.

Although few films based on biblical sources have
been made in the last ten years, a British producer,
John Heyman, has made a new version of Jesus' life
called simply Jesus, based entirely on Luke. "A film
for Bible purists," according to Time, it avoids subplots, Hollywood hype, and theorizing about Jesus'
motives. The film pays close attention to authenticity, with biblical scholars as consultants, and
all filming done in the Holy Land.[13] Miracles are
shown on camera. Time calls it less a "movie movie"
and more a documentary, which makes it sound like
Pasolini's film (I have not yet seen the film). Apparently, this is its weakness as well as its
strength. As in many books in the Bible, Luke's
emphasis is not on a flowing narrative, but on re-
cording the episodes in Jesus' life. There is no
attempt to connect the episodes, so any film faith-
fully following them is bound to lack unity and character development. Heyman is using the profits from
Jesus to finance a filming of the entire Bible which
he hopes to complete by the year 2000. This project
he intends to use for educational purposes, rather
than as a film to be shown in commercial theaters.

Even if we exclude Pasolini's and Heyman's films,
films based on the Bible have not been artistically
successful, and I have suggested some reasons why
these materials do not adapt easily to the screen.
If not artistically successful, however, Bible films
have been immensely popular. Kauffmann suggests this
popularity is just a sign of the spiritual emptiness
of our times; people who lack religious values attempt to find them in a DeMille epic:

> Possibly it is no coincidence that recent
> years, which are festooned with such ethical
> garlands as Bobby Baker's doings and mass

cheating at the Air Force Academy, have seen large audiences flocking to The Ten Commandments, Ben-Hur, King of Kings. One emptiness recognizes another.[14]

Ivan Butler takes a less elitist view, seeing these films as having considerable value:

> In particular regarding our perhaps somewhat jaundiced survey of the "religious spectacular," it is only fair to say that of all types of film this is one of the most difficult to bring off successfully in a commercial market. It must reimburse its generally enormous cost: so it must appeal to a mass audience. It has to feature one or more stars: so it has to be tailored to fit their personalities. It has to provide much superficially exciting action, so its stories must be elaborated or embellished. Throughout all the arts, myth, legend and story of early history have been similarly modified. Bearing in mind the additional difficulties and complexities with which the film has to contend, it is not remarkable that the still small voice is so seldom heard above the general din. The miracle is that, in spite of everything, such moments do occur; and this should be appreciated.[15]

Whatever the spiritual values biblical epics can provide, historical epics can give entertainment pleasures not found on television's small screen. No doubt this is why many Bible epics appeared in the 1950s when Americans were turning in large numbers to television. A well done epic film, or even a partial failure such as The Bible can give us the pleasures of the senses--of largeness and distance. It is partly this peculiar ability to show us the sweep of a scene and, in the case of historical films, to make us part of history, that makes epic films popular at the box office. Perhaps, as Pauline Kael says, we should be willing to override our prejudices and too-narrow theories about what the art of the film should be and refrain from judging epic films by the same standards as dramatic films.

On the other hand, movies based on biblical sources, whether done on an epic or more limited

scale <u>are</u> difficult to bring off. The brevity, simplicity, lack of characterization and coherent narrative flow pose immense problems for filmmakers. If a
director fills in, as DeMille and Stevens do in <u>The</u>
<u>Ten</u> <u>Commandments</u> and <u>The</u> <u>Greatest</u> <u>Story</u> <u>Ever</u> <u>Told</u>, he
is accused of distorting history and scripture, and
still his film will lack tight unity or character
development. If he tells the story straight as
Koster does in <u>David</u> <u>and</u> <u>Bathsheba</u>, he risks a plain,
dull film with thin content. The New Testament
offers more material, but again the lack of traditional narrative flow weakens unity. It appears the
quasi-documentary approach of Pasolini and Heyman is
best for lives of Jesus, but their faithful following
of Matthew and Luke poses problems also. Nevertheless, despite these problems and failures it is
likely that directors and producers will continue to
turn to the Bible for filmic materials, showing us
the powerful attraction the Bible still has for our
culture.

NOTES

[1] von Goethe, Johann Wolfgang, "On Epic and Dramatic Poetry," cited in Rudolf Arnheim, "Film Cul-
ture," in <u>Film</u>: <u>A</u> <u>Montage</u> <u>of</u> <u>Theories</u>, vol. 3, ed.
Richard Dyer MacCann (New York: Dutton, 1966),
p. 129.

[2] Henrietta Lehman, "The Ten Commandments," <u>Films</u>
<u>in</u> <u>Review</u>, 7, 9 (1956), 461.

[3] Bosley Crowther, cited in Gene Ringgold and
DeWitt Bodeen, <u>The</u> <u>Films</u> <u>of</u> <u>Cecil</u> <u>B</u>. <u>DeMille</u> (New
York: The Citadel Press, 1969), pp. 346-347.

[4] Cecil B. DeMille, <u>The</u> <u>Autobiography</u> <u>of</u> <u>Cecil</u> <u>B</u>.
<u>DeMille</u>, ed. Donald Hayne (Englewood Cliffs, N.J.:
Prentice-Hall, 1959), p. 399.

[5] Stanley Kauffmann, <u>A</u> <u>World</u> <u>on</u> <u>Film</u> (New York:
Harper & Row, 1966), p. 29.

[6] Pauline Kael, <u>Kiss</u> <u>Kiss</u> <u>Bang</u> <u>Bang</u> (Boston:
Little, Brown, 1968), p. 131.

[7]DeMille, p. 276.

[8]Mordaunt Hall, "Jesus of Nazareth," New York Times, 20 April 1927, p. 29, col. 2.

[9]Kauffmann, pp. 28-29

[10]Pier Paolo Pasolini, "An Epical-Religious View of the World," Film Quarterly, 18, 4 (Summer 1965), 34.

[11]Brendan Gill, "Seeking After A Sign," The New Yorker, 42, 2 (March 5, 1966), p. 157.

[12]Kael, p. 133.

[13]"A Film for Bible Purists," Time, 5 November 1979, p. 91.

[14]Kauffmann, p. 28.

[15]Ivan Butler, Religion in the Cinema (New York: A. S. Barnes, 1969), p. 202.

FLYING ELEPHANTS: TRANSFORMATIONS

IN LITERATURE AND FILM

Mark Harris

One of the most imaginative uses of the idea of film in literary fiction is Delmore Schwartz's story "In Dreams Begin Responsibilities" in which a young man is watching a movie that proves to depict the courtship of his mother and father. It's all very real to him, and in the theater he shouts out to them, telling them to stop, no good can come of it. Another patron of the theater becomes annoyed with him, telling him to be quiet, not to cry, this is only a movie. And the usher comes down the aisle with a flashlight and orders him to be silent or to leave.

The young man in the story has no name. Let's call him Delmore Schwartz. He has an artistic heart. In this characteristic, he resembles his mother. His father, on the other hand, is a very male, unartistic, antiartistic American. On the carousel in Schwartz's dream, father and mother ride round and round, trying for the nickel rings "attached to an arm of one of the posts." "My mother has acquired only two rings, my father, however, ten of them, although it was my mother who really wanted them." In this--in his greed, in his viewing a form of art merely as an opportunity--Schwartz's father is very much like a moving-picture producer. And it is the

producer, not the artist, who establishes the limits
to the art of making moving pictures.

Sometimes these limits are exceeded by some combination of artists working, often almost in a spirit
of conspiracy, who may make a classical or memorable
film, and who, when they do, do so almost by accident. When they are done they will hardly know how
they did it, nor will they ever be able to create
the conditions for doing it again.

The theorist, too, is caught up in this accident.
Theorists are conscious--or try to be--and they
therefore project consciousness upon producers,
thinking that the producer has done this or that for
reasons which must be known, at least to himself (or
herself). As often happens, in many fields, the
makers and the theorists are different people. In
either case, they may profit when they try to compre-
hend their opposites, but the producer meanwhile remains in a class of his own: his instinct is for the
economy, for the market, for the American box office
and the American public taste as they have evolved
at least since the advent of Jacksonian democracy;
he is the proprietor, boss, and ruler of a system
enclosed by his interpretation of the customer's desire. What does the customer want? The producer
tries it out on his spouse. What will the customer
go for? Best of all, from his point of view, he
tries it on himself only, flying by the seat of his
instincts. The director, who is an artist, may
fight for his right to the final cut of his film,
but the producer, who writes the checks, in one way
or another always retains the final cut for himself.

Thus Delmore Schwartz's father, walking in
Brooklyn to meet his future wife and to create the
author of the story, "jingles the coins in his pocket," and when "he becomes panicky about the bond already established" between his wife-to-be and himself, "he reassures himself by thinking of the big
men he admires who are married: William Randolph
Hearst and William Howard Taft."

We are conditioned. I am told that nobody has
insomnia in cultures where the mother carries the
baby on her back. As for me, I can sit immobilized
at a moving picture for hours. Almost no other action hypnotizes me in the same way--except, perhaps,
driving an automobile.

A great many events of my life that I thought I
had experienced I had actually experienced only at
the movies. For example, when, at age twenty, I was
drafted into the army, I was given a rifle and I set
about to shoot it. Until the moment I fired it I
believed I had fired it before. Now, when I fired
it, felt the recoil, heard the crashing report, and
smelled the burning powder, I realized that I had
never fired a rifle before, that I had only seen
rifles fired in many movie houses in Mt. Vernon,
New York. But my reaction to the sight, of course,
had carried such intensity and such conviction that
I thought I had done it myself. I got off easy.
Other boys, having seen exciting things in the movies, jumped off high buildings with umbrellas, thinking they would fly, or went off to the wars, which
in the movies looked so bloodless.

For Sam Johnson, weak eyes and all, the impact
of seeing exceeded the experiences of the other
senses. On April 10, 1783, Boswell introduced
Johnson to the Honorable and Reverend William Stuart.

> After some compliments on both sides, the
> tour which Johnson and I had made to the
> Hebrides was mentioned. JOHNSON. "I got an
> acquisition of more ideas by it than by any
> thing that I remember. I saw quite a differ-
> ent system of life." BOSWELL. "You would
> not like to make the same journey again?"
> JOHNSON. "Why no, Sir; not the same: it is
> a tale told. Gravina, an Italian critick,
> observes that every man desires to see that
> of which he has read; but no man desires to
> read an account of what he has seen: so much
> does description fall short of reality. De-
> scription only excites curiosity: seeing
> satisfies it. . . ."[1]

In Mt. Vernon, New York, we had a Loew's and a
Proctor's. These were chain theaters. We had a
double feature during the week and a single big feature Friday through Monday. There were several
smaller theaters--the Embassy, the Westchester, the
Bunny, the Parkway--but these smaller theaters were
theaters my mother warned me not to go to; bad things
happened there. But they were cheaper than the big
chain theaters, and I was tempted. Nothing bad ever

happened to me in a movie house, at least in the
sense in which my mother meant it. All that ever
happened to me in movie houses is that my mind was
formed, I was conditioned, my expectations were
shaped, I was programmed, I was brainwashed, my system of values was established almost beyond reform--
and my goals, my aspirations.

You and I, when we cast movies in our minds,
think who would be good for the part. The actor
gives the appearance of mattering most. He/she is
on all the talk shows, telling anecdotes about other
actors and actresses. The actor is the front for
the enterprise, the producer's slave, expendable,
with no life of his own until the producer produces
the conditions for work, whereupon the actor is pro-
moted to puppet. I heard on a talk show not long
ago that Vincent Price has never watched himself in
a movie. I like to think that this is his protest
against fragmentation. Given the fragmentary way in
which a movie is made--a few seconds at a time--the
emotion at which an actor is supposed to arrive may
be delayed for days or weeks. People who can in
this way display emotion on cue, who can work up
feeling promptly, or delay it indefinitely, have
either learned a complicated skill or come empty to
begin with.

Only the producer is whole. The musician, like
the actor, may be fragmented. The most successful
musician may be the composer who could never finish
anything: for the film producer he makes nine seconds
of music here, twelve seconds there.

As for the writer: my friend Stephen White, who
wrote for the movies, assured me that what was wanted
there was not talent but obedience. "Remember," he
said, "there's no such thing as a tenured screenwriter."

The American Constitution declares the separation
of church and state. In Mt. Vernon, New York, our
school system declared the separation of movies and
schools. If we saw a movie at school it had something to do with health or patriotism. I remember
one about tuberculosis and how not to contract it
(this seems odd to me now)--avoid tuberculosis by
not sharing another person's cigarette. Smoke your
own. When the movie showed someone with tuberculosis, a boy in our class named Arthur Taylor fainted.

The memory of the proper schooltime movie came back to me for The Southpaw. In this novel, Henry Wiggen, the baseball player, is a rookie at the training camp. The rookies are led to see an instructive movie. Nearly thirty years ago I think I captured fairly well the spirit of those films we often saw: commercial, heroic, ever-expanding America, land of wheels and smoke.

Then we seen this old-fashion sailboat, and people climbing a rock and cooking a turkey and fighting off the Indians, and later George Washington riding a big white horse whilst behind him come Americans in tatters and rags. Off in the distance we seen the British in red coats, for it was all in technicolor. The British looked tough, and myself I would of run like a bastard, but not Washington. He romped right up to them, and then the firing begun and the British went down like flies clutching their breast. Then shots of the war at New Orleans and Andrew Jackson on a white horse that looked like the same horse Washington had rode, and I said so to Perry and he laughed.
Between the various wars there was pictures of the map. First we was practically no bigger than Hungry or some such minor country, and then we took in all the territory out west. Then along come Abe Lincoln on an old-fashion train, writing down the Gettysburg address and then fading into smoke curling upwards from factories and the wheels all a-spinning and things coming off the factory lines that Perry said was like the Ford plant where he used to work in his summer vacations.
Soon come another war, and off went the marines, and they whipped them, the Spaniards I think. Who knows? And then another factory and more trains whizzing by, and cars on the highway--all Moors cars and shiny new Moors factories of course--and airplanes and the war in France and cannons, bombs and music.
Then there was some shots of Russia, and a more bedraggled lot of people you never

seen. There was 1 poor old woman with a hand-
kerchief around her head, walking along the
road and praying with her hands folded on her
breast. Then up behind her come a soldier on
a white horse, and it still looked like the
<u>same</u> <u>damn</u> <u>white</u> <u>horse</u> that Washington and
Jackson had rode, and I said so to Perry, and
he laughed again, and he come up behind this
lady and whipped out his sword and walloped
her over the head for no reason whatever.
When we come out it was raining. . . .[2]

Often when I arrived home from a moving picture
at Loew's or Proctor's or one of those other theaters
in Mt. Vernon, New York, I reviewed the film in my
mind and found the film wanting. Certain actions
had not been carried through, had not been concluded,
had just been stuck in but for some reason abandoned.

Then one evening at summer camp, I saw the movie
<u>Flying Elephants</u>, featuring Laurel and Hardy. Sum-
mer camp had movies. Summer camp was fun, unlike
school. School was health; summer camp was Laurel
& Hardy in a movie called <u>Flying Elephants</u>.

All I remember of the movie is the part where
the elephants flew. I was now at an age of reason,
trying to figure things out, and I must have been
struggling in my mind with the logic of storytelling.
I must have been thinking about form. In the film
Laurel said to Hardy, or Hardy said to Laurel--after
all those films I still don't know which was which,
like Bob and Ray, Huntley and Brinkley, but one said
to the other--"Look at that," pointing into the sky,
and then what we saw were two elephants flying past.

This had nothing to do with the plot of the movie. It had nothing to do with anything except my
future. Why were those flying elephants there? After a long time considering that question I arrived
at the answer that you may already have arrived at:
those flying elephants were there because somebody
had gone to the trouble of concocting some film showing elephants flying in the air, for what purpose we
shall never know. The moment to use it passed.

But the people who make movies--I mean the <u>pro-
ducers</u> of movies, not artists, not writers, not
directors, not actors, not designers, not theorists
--are not going to allow two flying elephants to go
to waste. The creative, inventive, imaginative

writer who thought up the brilliant idea of flying
elephants, the technical people (animal trainers,
for example, who taught the elephants to fly), the
director, and all other artists who participated in
this venture, having done their work, went on to new
realms of thought. But the producer watches the
money; he is accountable to himself and to others.
He is not Delmore Schwartz but Delmore Schwartz's
father, jingling coins in his pocket, and he is not
going to allow two elephants created by the resources of his company to fly away to another studio.

The producer cares nothing for story, for logic,
for form, for meaning, for history. The artist who
makes flying elephants exists at the mercy of the
producer. Luckily, these two flying elephants were
obviously useful, for here we are fifty years later
still talking about them. But the artist will be
dismissed who makes too many wasteful flying elephants. Things dangerous to business are not too
long tolerated where movies are made, as artists
have learned over time, of whom the best-known examples may be Charlie Chaplin and the blacklisted
Hollywood Ten.

The accidental nature of moviemaking was never
better expressed than by Susan Myrick in a letter to
Margaret Mitchell, as told in the book GWTW: The
Screenplay, which I derived from a review in
Smithsonian: "Producers and what they do with scripts
is like a chef making soup. . . . He tastes, adds
seasonings, tastes again, adds again. Perfect. Then
he does more things to it until he has the finest
soup in the universe. Whereupon, he calls in the
other chefs and they stand around and pee in it."

Accidents triumph over reason or plan. "I do
have the deepest respect for a dozen or so directors," John Cheever has said, "whose affairs are
centered there [in "Hollywood" so-called] and who,
in spite of the overwhelming problems of financing
films, continue to turn out brilliant and original
films." In the same mood, Irwin Shaw has said,
"When I first went out there at the age of twenty-
three, I had no illusions at all. I was almost as
cynical about Hollywood as you [an interviewer] seem
to be. Now after seeing all the good movies that
have been made since then, against all obstacles, I
have some hope for the movies, which is more than I
started out with."

The letter inviting me to this conference was
written on February 29, 1980. My late beloved agent,
Ad Schulberg, sometimes spoke of February 30, as if
February were a month like any other. She was of
the moving-picture family of the same name--B. P.
Schulberg, Budd Schulberg, and others--and of her
own maiden name, Jaffe. One of her first jobs in
movies fifty or sixty years ago was as a story editor: she often told me how she was summoned not to
a producer's bedside but to his table-side--his
massage table--to tell him the story of a recent
book. He had no personal plan to read that book.
Adeline read it for him. There he lay melting away
in his rubdown listening to, let us say, the story
of the latest Mary Roberts Rinehart book as interpreted by Adeline Schulberg. Listening for what?
Listening for its _elements_, rhyming with _elephants_,
some aspect of plot or character which lent itself
especially well to the resources and facilities of
his studio. What actors and actresses belong to
him? What friend's estate can he borrow as a location? Would he prefer to make a picture in cold
country or warm? What has he got left over from
last time? Can his writers write into Mary Roberts
Rinehart a couple of practically new flying elephants? Whom can he get? Whom does he hate? To
whom does he owe what?

Theme, meaning, point, purpose, moral intention,
political viewpoint, ethical outlook or philosophy
are irrelevant to the will of the producer seeking
the element, the bankable certainty, the customer's
desire. And when the producer says to the author,
"I loved your book," you know he means he loved it
as told to him by Ad Schulberg and fragmented for
his purpose.

Those of us who _think_ project thought. We at-
tribute order and plan to a process that is accidental, that enjoys only limited motion within a tightly
controlled procedure, employing toward that end mainly obedient people. I suppose it must be so. Making
a movie on location has the feeling of a military action, bullhorns and lines of supply, and shouted
commands, and life and death hanging on the technology.

And so we went through school in the age of film
and came out movie critics. But how can we be critics of the accidental? In the old days we reviewed

books.   The problem of movie criticism will never go
away until the Rorschach goes away, but the unconscious critic would improve himself/herself if he/
she would write film criticism in the form of film.
As things stand, he writes on paper. Now, when a
book reviewer writes on paper we can often see that
he writes poorly, and for that reason we discount
his remarks. Film critics should make films before
they criticize them. "One of the plagues of the
culture in which we live," writes Professor James
Ney in the journal Education, "is the verbosity of
those who don't, but know more than those who do--
one example is the music critics--another is the
literary critics. Such critics and their criticism
call to mind the complaints of the psychologist Leon
Jakobovitz who bewails the fact that the more powerfully correct theories don't work in the classroom
and that therefore, teachers, who are very practical
people, ignore them."
     Two young movie critics named Ebert and Siskel
conduct a program called "Sneak Previews" for
National Public Television. They do make a kind of
film of their criticism. The principal moment of
life to it on the night I watched it on PTV in
Phoenix, Arizona occurred when the two critics in
all their glee began to condemn pictures they called
"dogs." What was lively was not their commentary
but the fact of their bringing an actual dog before
the camera, and the dog jumped around a good bit and
was amusing as dogs can be in the absence of more
substantial activity. I am sure these critics would
like to make movies, but they haven't had the chance.
Their frustration turns to bitterness, and they begin to try to account for the "success" or "failure"
of films in terms that would be much more realistic
if they really would drop everything, leave their
dog at home, start at the very beginning of the
moviemaking process, and see how far they can go.
     Try to find a good script to start with. Try to
find people to support the script with money. All
you need to make a modest movie is a few million
dollars. Who will give it to you? And what will
they want from you in return?
     The quest for money will be immensely instructive
for all aspects of moviemaking. That which was formerly an idle phrase now comes vividly to life in all
colors: "controlling interest."

Let us say you have in your mind a wonderful
story you want to make a movie of. You also have in
mind one or two outstanding actors or actresses to
play the primary roles. You also have in mind a
director, a location, and other important features.
You can see yourself there. You visualize a beautiful film, a masterpiece, a classic. It will make its
participants rich, and you are running through your
mind the modest remarks that you, as creator, intend
to make on that most discouraging night of the year
--the night of the Academy Awards. With the few
million dollars you raised (I don't know how) you
inherited a few million problems, too, step-by-step,
day-by-day, detail-by-detail, phone call-by-phone
call, person-by-person, none of which is going to be
apparent to two rather self-satisfied innocent young
men calling themselves critics and sitting in a
studio in Chicago with a dog.

Many critics employ the terms and jargon of the
moviemaking trade to give the impression of knowledge
or awareness, as if by the blessings of nomenclature
they have an inside track on judgment--jump cut and
angle shots, back projections and crosscuts, dissolves and dolly shots, wipes and zooms. We novelists know this fictional trick of employing the language of special knowledge to present the illusion
that our created character is terribly close to the
subject.

But the critic is really as innocent as you or I,
or more so. I at least think I know how I got this
way, how I almost fooled myself into believing I
could make play look like work. I wanted to be a
success at something besides dreaming of naked la-
dies. Soon it occurred to me to do what people told
me I had a certain talent for--to write things up,
be a journalist, a storyteller, go in for literature.
It never occurred to me that literature, which I
associated with books and school and health and patriotism, was in any way connected with movies, which
meant fun and summer camp, or total, blissful absorp-
tion in a dark room. Novels were respectable. Movies were not. Nobody told me that novels themselves
had once been contraband. Then I learned, in spite
of school, that novels and novel-writing were really
play; my life's work could be play. In time, the
names of some things changed but the principle re-
mained. The moving picture assumed the status of the

novel. It became respectable. People began to take
movies seriously. My friend whose parents took him
to the movies for the education of it was no longer
an outlaw. I had always thought that going to the
movies was a special event, it was something you did
only on weekends--it was nothing you ever did on
"school nights" when you were obliged to get up early
the next morning. It was an act of the purest de-
light, possibly because it was not in any way connected with school or schoolwork--it was the antith-
esis of school, it was separated from school, it was
pure pleasure--unlike school, which was where one
went to be judged or reprimanded.

    But now movies are joined to school, we are see-
ing movies as part of our academic work, and we are
writing about movies as if they were important
events, like the Phoenician wars. The other side of
our self-indulgence is our puritanism. We are very
guilty about having turned work into fun, about
studying movies--a contradiction in terms--and so we
pretend that we are working very hard at trying to
assess and analyze and understand films. One of my
sons takes a course in film. The course is called
a laboratory, as if he is a scientist.

    At many universities, big film courses pay the
bills as big mass freshman English courses formerly
paid the bills, or as Psychology 1 did--that big mass
course where a professor whose name I have forgotten
pointed out to me something I mentioned earlier this
evening--that many events of my life which I thought
I had seen I had actually experienced only at the
movies.

    And so we are warned before we begin. Even so,
of course, against all obstacles, as Irwin Shaw puts it,
moviemakers do begin. They are aware of all "the
more powerfully correct theories"; they have not yet
been overwhelmed by the reality of accident; they
proceed as if it were all quite rational and possible, and sometimes they enjoy something like success.
And what is true for the moviemaker has always been
true for the writer--this is where I get the chance
to use my subtitle, "Transformations in Literature
and Film"--and may for all I know be true as well for
every kind of artist in every art, for the writer
whose successes are as inexplicable to himself or
herself as his or her so-called failures, whose failures seem often to be superior to his or her suc-

cesses. William Gibson, a writer of extraordinary
prose whose work you will know by its so-called successes (The Miracle Worker, Two for the Seesaw) asked
me once if I had considered the fact that most of
what we do is "debacle." In a letter in December,
1977, just after "this debacle with Golda" (a play
which could not fail, with William Gibson playwright,
Arthur Penn directing, and Anne Bancroft as Golda
Meir--a play that failed all the same), he wrote,
"Well, debacle, I'll earn a good year's salary out of
it, and I've had debacles where I earned chiefly a
hemorrhage. . . . And Bill Inge killed himself because of his debacles, and Tennessee Williams hasn't
had a success in fifteen years, and Arthur Miller
after two recent flops is said to be tending his
apple orchard. . . ."
　　Luckily, the writer of literature--books--can
function in solitude, apart from the producer. Where
reason seems submerged, and in the absence of his own
chance for influence, the writer remains at home.
This is my message--off the ground at last! In the
presence of the moving picture, abandon yourself to
the subjective state. Abandon puritanism. Abandon
science--the moviehouse is a moviehouse, not a laboratory; movies are made by accident, play is play.
With Cheever and Irwin Shaw, take the happy accidents
as they come. And if the moving picture had never
been invented, I should simply have said this of literature.

NOTES

[1]Boswell's Life of Johnson (Oxford University
Press, 1953), p. 1218.
　　[2]Mark Harris, The Southpaw (Bobbs-Merrill, 1953),
pp. 92-93.

INDEX